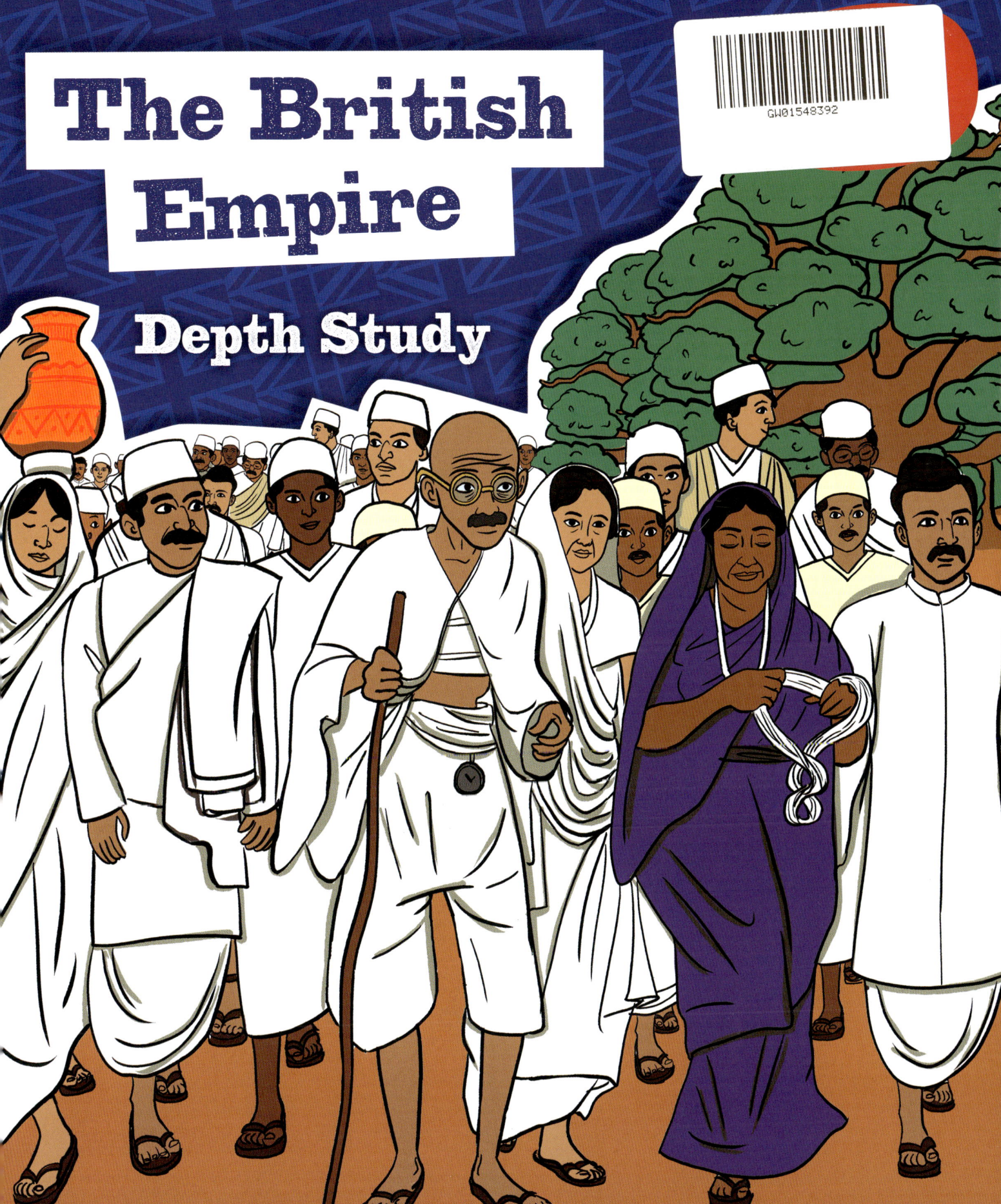

OXFORD
UNIVERSITY PRESS

Great Clarendon Street, Oxford, OX2 6DP, United Kingdom

Oxford University Press is a department of the University of Oxford. It furthers the University's objective of excellence in research, scholarship, and education by publishing worldwide. Oxford is a registered trade mark of Oxford University Press in the UK and in certain other countries.

© Oxford University Press 2023

The moral rights of the author have been asserted

First published in 2023

All rights reserved. No part of this publication may be reproduced, stored in a retrieval system, or transmitted, in any form or by any means, without the prior permission in writing of Oxford University Press, or as expressly permitted by law, by licence or under terms agreed with the appropriate reprographics rights organization. Enquiries concerning reproduction outside the scope of the above should be sent to the Rights Department, Oxford University Press, at the address above.

You must not circulate this work in any other form and you must impose this same condition on any acquirer.

British Library Cataloguing in Publication Data
Data available

978-1-382-04236-9

978-1-382-04234-5 (ebook)
978-1-382-04235-2 (Kerboodle digital book)

10 9 8 7 6 5 4 3 2

MIX
Paper | Supporting responsible forestry
FSC® C007785

The manufacturing process conforms to the environmental regulations of the country of origin.

Printed in the United Kingdom by Bell & Bain

Acknowledgements
The publisher would like to thank the following for permissions to use copyright material:

The Liverpool Echo: Extract from an article 'Story of city's past is written in stone'; The Liverpool Echo, 14 AUG 2007. Reprinted by permission from Reach Licensing/ mirrorpix. **William Dalrymple:** Extract from an article 'The East India Company: The original corporate raiders' by William Dalrymple; The Guardian on 4 March 2015. Reprinted by permission from Guardian News & Media Limited. **Shashi Tharoor:** Tweet by Shashi Tharoor on Twitter; 12 June 2020. Courtesy of Dr. Sashi Tharoor. **William Dalrymple and Anita Anand:** A podcast text from William Dalrymple talking with Anita Anand in Episode 2 'Company Rule in India' on the Empire podcast series in 2022; Goalhanger Podcasts. Used by permission from the publisher 'Goalhanger Podcasts'. **Jan Morris:** Adapted from 'Pax Britannica' by Jan Morris (1968) Faber & Faber. Copyright © 1968 Jan Morris. Reprinted by permission from United Agents LLP. **Shashi Tharoor:** Adapted extract from an article "But what about the railways ...?' The myth of Britain's gifts to India' written by Shashi Tharoor; The Guardian on 8 March 2017. Reprinted by permission from Guardian News & Media Limited. **Aaron Wilkes:** From a leaflet written in 1907 by Indians in Bengal from the book 'British out KS3 GCSE History 4e Technology, War and Independence: 1901-Present Day'; OUP 2020. Copyright © 2020 Aaron Wilkes. **Aina J Khan and Thaslima Begum:** An extract from a 2022 interview with Zareena Parveen "A Sikh soldier pulled me out of the rubble': survivors recall India's violent partition – and reflect on its legacy'; The Guardian Thu 11 Aug 2022. Reprinted by permission from Guardian News & Media Limited. **Geneva Abdul:** An extract from the article 'Uprooted by partition: 'I feel I don't belong in England. I'm a very proud Punjabi' by Geneva Abdul; The Guardian Mon 15 Aug 2022. Reprinted by permission from Guardian News & Media Limited. **Thomas Mayor:** An extract from the article 'We learnt early that white ghosts can lie. Australians are ready for truth and reckoning' written by Thomas Mayor; The Guardian Fri 20 May 2022. Reprinted by permission from Guardian News & Media Limited. **Gordon Syron and Elaine Syron:** A quote from Uncle Gordon Syron, Worimi, Birpai, 2009. Copyright © 2009 Gordon Syron and Elaine Syron. Reprinted by permission from the author. Professor Saul David: A quote from Telegraph article by Charlotte Edwardes - "Wrong men", published on 19 October 2003, The Telegraph. Reprinted by permission from The Telegraph. **David Olusoga:** An extract from the article 'Wake up, Britain: Should the empire really be a source of pride?' written by David Olusoga; The Guardian Sat 23 Jan 2016. Reprinted by permission from Guardian News & Media Limited. **Sathnam Sanghera:** A extract from an interview with Ellie Cawthorne - History Extra magazine, 29 November 2021. Copyright © 2021 Sathnam Sanghera. Used with permissions from History Extra magazine. **Paul Kane and Molly Groarke:** An extract from article - 'British Empire Facts' published by the National Geographic Kids. Copyright © Paul Kane and Molly Groarke. **Catherine Hall:** Adapted from 'Culture and Identity in Imperial Britain' by Catherine Hall. Published in Sarah Stockwell (ed.) The British Empire. Themes and Perspectives (2008). Copyright © 2008, John Wiley and Sons. Used by permission from the arrangement of Copyright Clearance Centre. **Imperial War Museum:** A text extract from video called 'What role did the British Empire play in the Second World War? Did Britain really stand alone?'. Copyright © Imperial War Museums. Used permission from IWM. **Siya Mnyanda:** An extract from the article 'Cecil Rhodes' colonial legacy must fall – not his statue' written by Sian Mnyanda; The Guardian Wed 25 Mar 2015. Reprinted by permission from Guardian News & Media Limited.

The publisher and authors would like to thank the following for permission to use photographs and other copyright material:

Cover illustration: Chanté Timothy / Darley Anderson Illustration Agency

Artwork by Q2A Media, Abel Ippolito, Moreno Chiacchiera, Rudolf Farkas, Martin Sanders & Oxford University Press.

Photos: p6(l): AF Fotografie / Alamy Stock Photo; **p7(tl):** Photo 12 / Alamy Stock Photo; **p7(ml):** Tim Ring / Alamy Stock Photo; **p7(tr):** Noppadonkoko / Shutterstock; **p11(t):** PA Images / Alamy Stock Photo; **p11(b):** The History Collection / Alamy Stock Photo; **p15(l):** Chaitanyo / Alamy Stock Photo; **p15(r):** Florilegius / Alamy Stock Photo; **p16:** The Picture Art Collection / Alamy Stock Photo; **p17:** Raymond Tang / Alamy Stock Photo; **p18:** incamerastock / Alamy Stock Photo; **p19:** GRANGER - Historical Picture Archive / Alamy Stock Photo; **p22:** Yuriy Boyko_Ukraine/Shutterstock; **p24:** Lebrecht Music & Arts / Alamy Stock Photo; **p27:** John Davidson Photos / Alamy Stock Photo; **p27(inset):** marc zakian 2 / Alamy Stock Photo; **p29(l):** DnDavis/Shutterstock; **p29(r):** Science History Images / Alamy Stock Photo; **p30:** The Picture Art Collection / Alamy Stock Photo; **p32:** The Royal Mint; **p33:** Georgios Kollidas / Alamy Stock Photo; p34: SBS Eclectic Images / Alamy Stock Photo; p35(t): AF Fotografie / Alamy Stock Photo; **p35(b):** The Trustees of the British Museum; **p37(tl):** Travel Wild / Alamy Stock Photo; **p37(tr):** Dinodia Photos / Alamy Stock Photo; **p37(bl):** Boris Stroujko / Shutterstock; p37(br): Nataliya Davidovich / Alamy Stock Photo; **p38:** World History Archive / Alamy Stock Photo; **p39:** Andrew Wood / Alamy Stock Photo; **p40:** Ivan Vdovin / Alamy Stock Photo; **p41:** Krupasindhu Muduli/Wikimedia Commons; p42: Everett Collection Historical / Alamy Stock Photo; **p43:** Well/BOT / Alamy Stock Photo; **p45:** The Print Collector / Alamy Stock Photo; **p46:** CPA Media Pte Ltd / Alamy Stock Photo; **p47:** British Library Board. All Rights Reserved / Bridgeman Images; **p48:** PA Images / Alamy Stock Photo; **p49(l):** Vintage_Space / Alamy Stock Photo; **p49(r):** Historic Collection / Alamy Stock Photo; **p50:** Photo 12 / Alamy Stock Photo; **p52:** PA Images / Alamy Stock Photo; p54: mauritius images GmbH / Alamy Stock Photo; **p55:** Pictorial Press Ltd / Alamy Stock Photo; **p56:** NDK / Alamy Stock Photo; **p58:** Leigh Henningham / Alamy Stock Photo; p59(l): Sydney Parkinson (artist), Thomas Chambers/British Library; p59(r): Universal Images Group North America LLC / Alamy Stock Photo; **p60:** Joe / Alamy Stock Photo; **p61(l):** Chronicle / Alamy Stock Photo; **p61(r):** Mary Evans Picture Library; **p62:** Gordon Syron and Elaine Syron; p63: Historic Collection / Alamy Stock Photo; **p65(t):** The AGE/Fairfax Media via Getty Images via Getty Images; **p65(ml):** Richard H Heyes / Alamy Stock Vector; **p65(mr):** Zoonar GmbH / Alamy Stock Photo; **p65(b):** Fir Mamat / Alamy Stock Photo; **p66:** IanDagnall Computing / Alamy Stock Photo; **p67:** Peter Probst / Alamy Stock Photo; p68(l): Zoonar GmbH / Alamy Stock Photo; **p68(m):** Richard H Heyes / Alamy Stock Vector; **p68(r):** Peter Probst / Alamy Stock Photo; **p70(t):** Prachaya Roekdeethaweesab/ Shutterstock; **p70(b):** CBW / Alamy Stock Photo; **p71:** The History Collection / Alamy Stock Photo; **p72:** GRANGER - Historical Picture Archive / Alamy Stock Photo; **p73:** Geopix / Alamy Stock Photo; **p74(l):** History and Art Collection / Alamy Stock Photo; **p74(r):** © IWM HU 58315; **p75(t):** CBW / Alamy Stock Photo; **p75(b):** Chronicle / Alamy Stock Photo; **p77(t):** Public Domain; **p77(b):** incamerastock / Alamy Stock Photo; **p78:** Ian Nellist / Alamy Stock Photo; **p79:** Science History Images / Alamy Stock Photo; **p82:** Pictorial Press Ltd / Alamy Stock Photo; **p83(t):** Science History Images / Alamy Stock Photo; **p83(b):** Photo 12 / Alamy Stock Photo; **p86(t):** Iconpix / Alamy Stock Photo; **p86(b):** Andreas von Einsiedel / Alamy Stock Photo; **p87:** IanDagnall Computing / Alamy Stock Photo; **p88:** CBW / Alamy Stock Photo; **p89:** World History Archive / Alamy Stock Photo; **p91(l):** National Archives Ghana Search Room at PRAAD; **p91(r):** Anonymous/AP/Shutterstock; **p92(t):** Sopotnicki/Shutterstock; **p92(b):** National Army Museum; **p93:** Hoberman Publishing / Alamy Stock Photo; **p94:** Science History Images / Alamy Stock Photo; **p95:** Ian Nellist / Alamy Stock Photo; **p96:** EggImages / Alamy Stock Photo; **p97:** Chronicle of World History / Alamy Stock Photo; **p98:** Tim Ring / Alamy Stock Photo; **p99(l):** Muhammed Furqan / Alamy Stock Photo; **p99(r):** Tony Watson / Alamy Stock Photo; **p100:** PA Images / Alamy Stock Photo; **p101:** Imagedoc / Alamy Stock Photo.

Although we have made every effort to trace and contact all copyright holders before publication this has not been possible in all cases. If notified, the publisher will rectify any errors or omissions at the earliest opportunity.

From the author: Aaron would like to thank the fantastic Polly Coupar-Hennessy, Beth Kamen and Alison Schrecker at Oxford University Press for their tireless hard work, practical suggestions and infectious enthusiasm at every stage of this project. In addition, I would like to credit the help and sound advice of Sarah Flynn, Shalina Patel, Rob Bircher, Kate Buckley and all the expert historians, academics and teachers we have consulted. Finally, of course, I am particularly indebted to the people who support me at home. Without their kind words, patience, encouragement, cake, tea and biscuits, it would have been impossible for me to write this book.

The publisher would like to thank the following people for offering their contribution in the development of this book: Shalina Patel, David Rawlings, Daniel Aspinall, Tamsin Shelton and James Helling. Relevant sections have also been reviewed by Dr Lauren Working (University of York), Anindita Ghosh (Professor of Modern Indian History, University of Manchester), Dr James Boyce (Historian and Author, University of Tasmania), James McDougall (Professor of Modern and Contemporary History, University of Oxford), Dr Natasha Robinson (School of Education, University of Bristol) and Dr Emily Manktelow (Senior Lecturer in Global and Colonial History, Royal Holloway University of London). We are very grateful for their careful reviews and valuable input.

Contents

Introducing KS3 History: British Empire 4
Timeline of the British Empire 6

Big Question 1: What is an empire? 8
Big Question 2: Why is it important to study the British Empire? 10
Big Question 3: Why did Britain want an empire? 12

Chapter 1: British America
1.1	What was North America like before the British arrived?	14
1.2 A/B	How did the British Empire begin?	16
1.3 A/B	Life in the colonies	20
1.4 A/B	Britain and the trade in enslaved Africans	24
1.5	Revolution	28
1	Have you been learning?	30

Big Question 4: Why was the trade in enslaved Africans abolished in the British Empire? 32

Chapter 2: British India
2.1	What was India like before the British invaded?	36
2.2	The invasion of India	38
2.3	The end of Company rule	40
2.4	The First War of Independence	42
2.5	What was the impact of the empire on Britain and India?	44
2.6 A/B	Independence for India	46
2.7	The Partition of India	50
2	Have you been learning?	52

Big Question 5: How did the British Empire change Britain at the time? 54

Chapter 3: Australia
3.1	What was Australia like before the British arrived?	56
3.2	Finding *Terra Australis Incognita*	58
3.3	Who were the 'first fleeters'?	60
3.4 A/B	The colonisation of Australia	62
3.5	An independent Australia	66
3	Have you been learning?	68

Big Question 6: How did people resist colonisation? 70
Big Question 7: How did the empire help win two world wars? 74

Chapter 4: The British in Africa
4.1	Africa and its kingdoms	78
4.2	The invasion of Africa	80
4.3 A/B/C	The Anglo-Zulu War	82
4.4	How did a war in Africa change British schools?	88
4.5 A/B	Independence in Africa	90
4	Have you been learning?	94

Big Question 8: How and why have views on the British Empire changed? 96
Big Question 9: What is the legacy of the British Empire? 98

Glossary 102
Index 103

Introducing KS3 History: British Empire

What is this book about?

This textbook covers a period in history when Britain controlled lots of land in different parts of the world. Collectively, the land was known as the British Empire. It doesn't actually exist any more, but at its height it was the largest empire the world had ever seen. It lasted over 400 years and spanned many of the periods of history that you will have studied – the Tudor, Stuart, Georgian and Victorian periods, for example.

The first small steps in building the British Empire were taken during the reign of Henry VII – the father of Henry VIII. It began to expand during Elizabeth I's reign, at the time of the Spanish Armada and William Shakespeare. It continued to grow at the time of the Gunpowder Plot and the English Civil War, and it grew further during the era of the industrial revolution. It reached its height in the period between the two world wars, and began its decline after the Second World War. In fact, it lasted right up to the time when Elizabeth II (reigned 1952–2022) was queen.

Many historians have studied the British Empire. In the past, a great deal was written from a British point of view and there was a belief that the empire was making a positive impact on the places it controlled. However, in recent years there has been more focus on the idea that the wealth and power that Britain achieved as it built its empire came at a price – and this price was largely paid by the local people whose land the British invaded.

Using this book

This book will get you thinking. Some of the things you look at will challenge you. Some things might really surprise (or even shock) you, or get you thinking in a different way. You will be asked to look at different pieces of evidence and to try to work things out for yourself. Sometimes, two pieces of evidence about the same event won't agree with each other. You might be asked to think of reasons why that is. Your answers might not be the same as your friend's or even your teacher's. This is okay. The important thing is to give reasons for your thoughts and ideas, as you examine, question and try to understand the full story of this important part of world history.

Getting the history right

We have consulted lots of experts to ensure that the content of this book is as accurate as possible and reflects the latest 'historical scholarship' (historians writing about history). Historians who have helped us include Dr Lauren Working (University of York), Anindita Ghosh (Professor of Modern Indian History, University of Manchester), Dr James Boyce (Historian and Author, University of Tasmania), James McDougall (Professor of Modern and Contemporary History, University of Oxford), Dr Natasha Robinson (School of Education, University of Bristol) and Dr Emily Manktelow (Senior Lecturer in Global and Colonial History, Royal Holloway University of London). We've also worked with teachers including Shalina Patel, one of the leading teachers in the study of the British Empire in schools.

There's another thing that's important to mention when we study the British Empire – the story isn't fixed. It is constantly developing as historians think more deeply about empire and uncover rich stories about the people who lived in it. In short, this textbook is a work in progress!

Also, we have had to make difficult decisions about what we leave out. We can't include every detail of every part of the empire story – but I hope we've managed to show you a thorough picture and made room for the Indigenous populations of the colonies to share their stories and explain the impact of empire on their lives.

Aaron Wilkes

Key features

Key Words These are important words and terms that are vital to your understanding of the topic. You can spot them easily because they are in bold red type. Look up their meanings in the glossary at the back of the book.

Connections This gives you an idea of what is happening in other parts of the world, at the same time as the period you are studying. It will help you draw parallels between the topic you are currently studying and other historical topics.

Objectives All lessons in this book start by setting you objectives. These are your key aims setting out your learning targets for the work ahead.

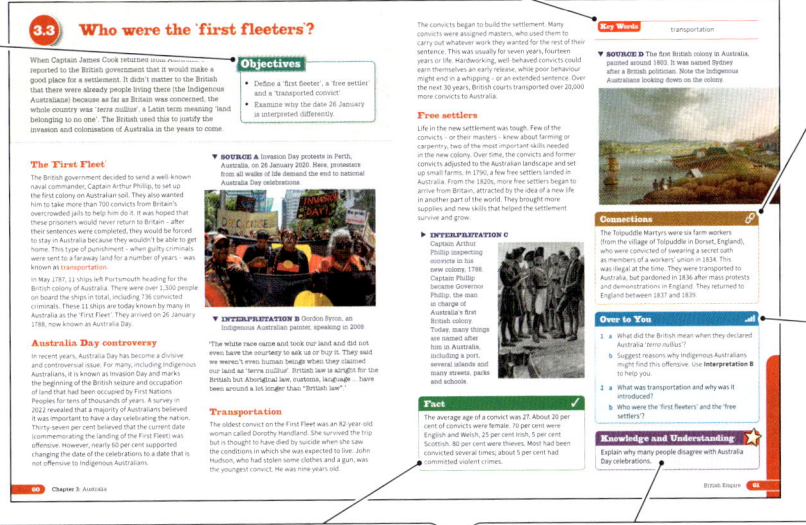

Over to You These activities are an opportunity for you to demonstrate your knowledge and understanding. The tasks become progressively more challenging.

Fact These are fascinating little bits of history that you don't usually hear about! They give you extra insights into topics and challenge the way you think.

History Skills These activities test a range of history skills, so each box has its own title. The tasks will challenge you to think a little deeper about what you have been studying. These are also important skills to develop if you are going to study GCSE History.

Big Question You will come across some 'Big Questions' about the British Empire. These will make you think really hard about some of the big ideas, themes and questions related to the British Empire.

Earlier on… / Meanwhile… / Later on…  You will be challenged to think how the topic relates to events, people, ideas or developments that may have taken place years before, at the same time, or years later.

Have you been learning?

There are different types of assessments at the end of every chapter. These are opportunities for you to showcase what you have learned and to put your ability to recall key information and demonstrate history skills to the test.

 Quick Knowledge Quiz These short tests will give you a quick snapshot of what you have remembered about the chapter.

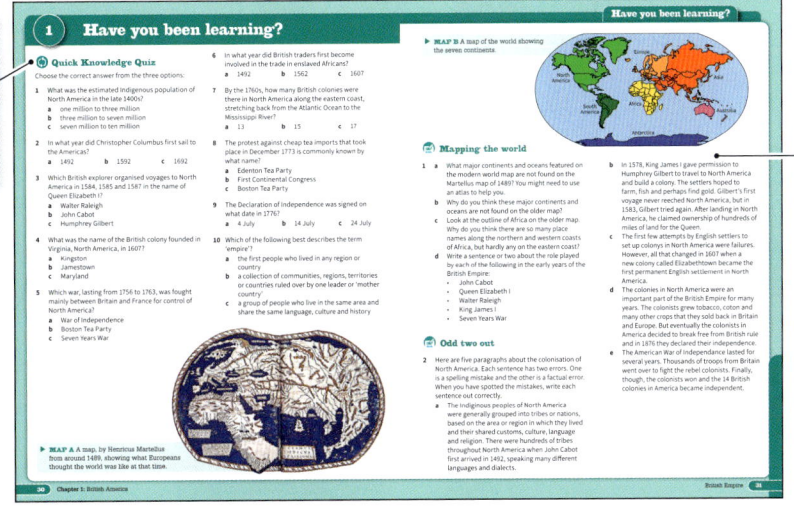

In-depth activities These activities will test your knowledge and understanding of the chapter in more depth. They will also help you develop key literacy skills such as making inferences and writing in detail.

British Empire

Timeline of the British Empire

The British Empire lasted for over 400 years. From small beginnings in the 1500s, the British Empire grew to become the largest empire the world had ever known. It was even bigger than the Roman Empire. The timeline on this page shows some of the big events, significant people and changes that took place at this time.

KEY
- British America
- British India
- Australia
- Africa
- Big Question

Fact ✓

Some historians split the era of the British Empire into two phases. The first phase (the 'First British Empire') is the time England invaded North America and parts of the Caribbean, and set up trading areas in India and expanded its territory there. It ended when the United States broke away from Britain after they won the American War of Independence. The 'Second British Empire' covers the foundation of colonies in places such as Australia, New Zealand and large parts of Africa. The British government also took more direct control over India.

1881
The partition of Africa begins that sees the invasion and colonisation of most of Africa by Britain and other European powers

1857–1858
Indian Rebellion results in India coming under the formal control of the British government

1833
The Slavery Abolition Act bans the enslavement of people in the British Empire

1801
Act of Union unites Britain and Ireland

1788
The first ships carrying convicted criminals from England arrive in Australia

1562
John Hawkins transports enslaved Africans to Spanish colonies, starting British involvement in the trade in enslaved Africans

1600
Formation of the East India Company

1655
The island of Jamaica is taken from the Spanish and becomes part of the Empire

1497
John Cabot sent by King Henry VII on an expedition to find a route to Asia via the Atlantic. He lands on the coast of Newfoundland, in what we now call Canada

1607
First English settlement (Jamestown) on the mainland of North America. British colonisation in North America involves the seizure of territory from Indigenous Americans

1899–1902
The Second Anglo-Boer War is fought between Dutch settlers (the Boers) and the British

1947
British-controlled India gains independence and is partitioned (split) into the nations of India and Pakistan

1980
The last British colony becomes independent (Zimbabwe)

1952
Mau Mau Rebellion breaks out in opposition to British rule in Kenya

1957
The Gold Coast (as it was known under British rule) becomes the independent state of Ghana

1948
British Nationality Act passed, which makes all people living in Commonwealth countries British citizens. This meant they could have a British passport and the right to move to Britain

1770
Captain James Cook reaches Australia and claims 'New South Wales' for Britain

1775
The American War of Independence breaks out (and lasts until 1783)

1757
British victory at the Battle of Plassey allows the East India Company to take over Bengal, one of the richest parts of India

Over to You

1. Working out which year is in which century can be tricky. The easiest way is to cover up the last two numbers in a year and add 1 to the first two numbers. For example, 1757 is in the eighteenth century (cover up the '57' and add 1 to 17 to make 18). Which century are the following years in?
   - **a** 1788
   - **b** 1948
   - **c** 1562
   - **d** 1881
   - **e** 1600

2. Which century were the following events in?
   - **a** The American War of Independence
   - **b** The Partition of India
   - **c** John Cabot's expedition for Henry VII
   - **d** The formation of the East India Company
   - **e** The Act of Union that united Britain and Ireland

3. Now put the five events above in the correct chronological order.

British Empire

Big Question 1: What is an empire?

Empires have existed for many thousands of years. Many of you reading this now will have probably studied one or two empires already – the Romans perhaps, or the Maya, or the Aztecs. The Egyptians had a sort of empire too. So, what exactly is an empire?

Objectives
- Define key terms such as 'empire', 'colony' and 'Indigenous'.
- Identify reasons why countries build empires.

Empire explained

An empire is a collection of communities, regions, territories, states or even countries that are ruled over and controlled by one leader or 'mother country'. The areas controlled by the 'mother country' are usually called colonies. However, they are sometimes called protectorates, dominions or dependencies. The 'mother country' then makes many (or sometimes all) of the key decisions to do with the places it rules over.

How does a country get an empire?

Empires are mostly built by force. A rich, powerful country takes control of other, less powerful countries or regions – perhaps after defeating them in a war, to gain access to their resources, or to stop rival 'empire-builders' from getting there first. The 'mother country' rules over its colonies to benefit itself; the rights and needs of the colonies are frequently overlooked or ignored. In some cases, empire-building is more brutal than this, resulting in the mistreatment, enslavement or destruction of the Indigenous peoples who were living there long before their region or country was invaded.

Fact ✓
The process of taking control over a region and/or the Indigenous peoples of an area is known as 'colonisation'. When control has been established, the area and people are said to be 'colonised'.

Why do some countries want empires?

There are lots of reasons why some countries try to take over others. After a war, the winning nation may take over the defeated one and include it in their empire. Other countries go 'empire-hunting' because they want more resources like grain, cattle, gold, silver, tin or iron. They take over other countries to steal all the things they want. Sometimes countries have even taken over territory just to stop rival powerful nations getting it first. Countries have also invaded others because they wrongly felt they had a 'right' to the land, or felt they were superior to the Indigenous peoples already living there.

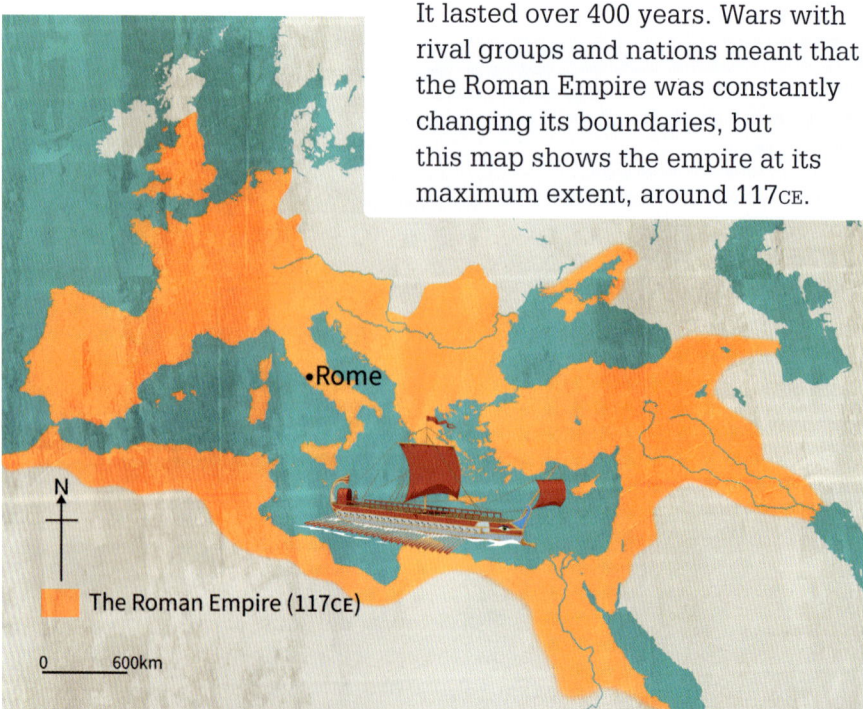

▼ **MAP A** The Romans built their empire gradually from about 27 BCE. It lasted over 400 years. Wars with rival groups and nations meant that the Roman Empire was constantly changing its boundaries, but this map shows the empire at its maximum extent, around 117 CE.

The Roman Empire (117 CE)
0   600km

The rise and fall of empires

Over many thousands of years there have been many different empires. There are some very famous ones (like the Roman, Inca and Aztec empires) but lots of other civilisations and countries have had empires at one time or another too. The list includes the Egyptians, Persians, Greeks, Portuguese, French, Russians, Turks, Austrians, Chinese and Japanese. Often (but not always) each empire has ended because they have been defeated by a fresh, powerful, 'up-and-coming' country, which takes its place as the world's most powerful 'empire nation'. In other cases, empires have ended because of resistance from groups or nations that refused to be colonised.

The largest empire in the world

One country not mentioned so far is Britain. From small beginnings in the early 1600s, Britain's empire grew and grew. By 1900, land nearly 40 times the size of Britain itself was part of the British Empire. Britain ruled over 400 million people living in 56 different places all over the world. This amounted to approximately one-quarter of the world's population and one-quarter of the Earth's total land area.

However, around 50 years later, after two world wars, more and more countries wanted their independence and caused the British Empire to begin to break apart.

Big Question

Key Words mother country   colony   protectorate   dominion   dependency   Indigenous peoples   superior

Over to You

1 a In your own words, explain what is meant by the terms 'empire', 'colony' and 'colonisation'.

   b Why do you think the term 'mother country' is sometimes used when describing empire nations?

   c What are the main methods nations used to build empires?

2 a Write down the subtitle 'The British Empire' and then write down five pieces of information or facts about it.

   b Look at **Map B**. Can you name any of the countries that were once part of the British Empire (coloured in pink)?

Cause

Describe two reasons why some countries built up empires.

▶ **MAP B** This map shows the extent of the Spanish Empire in the 1500s, when it was one of the largest empires in the world and took over two other empires – the Inca and Aztec empires of Central and South America. You can also see the extent of the British Empire in 1900.

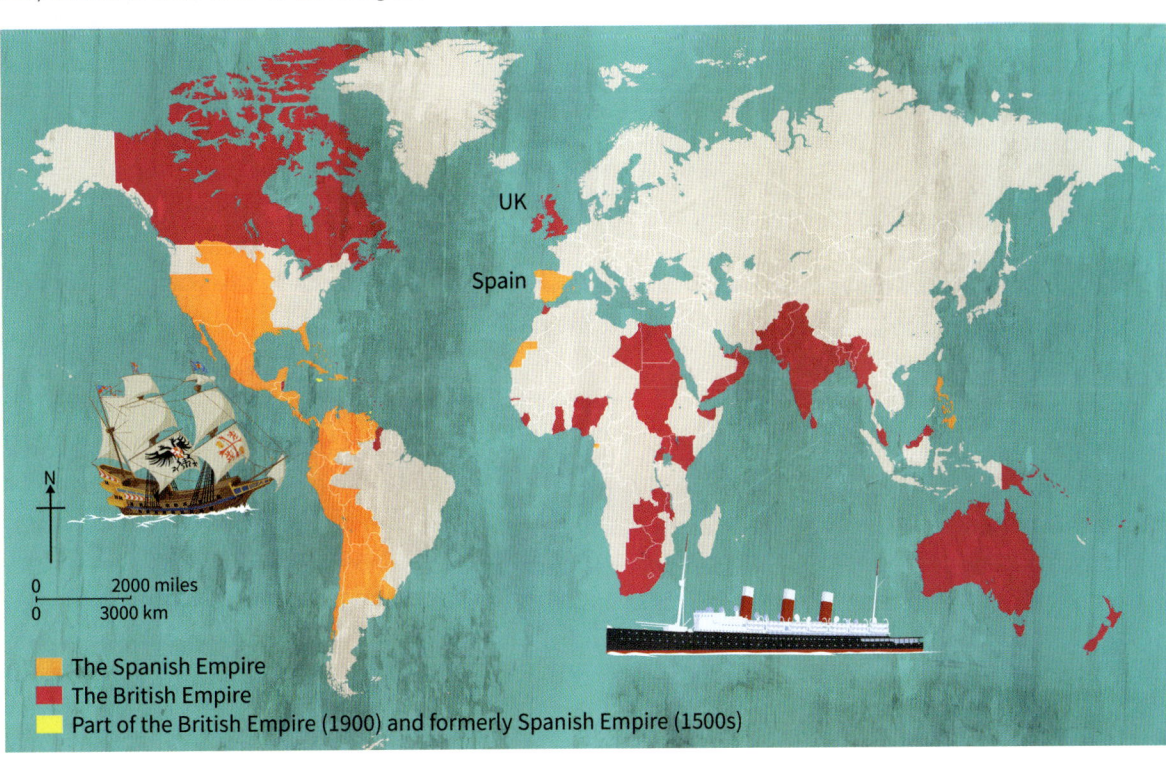

- 🟧 The Spanish Empire
- 🟥 The British Empire
- 🟨 Part of the British Empire (1900) and formerly Spanish Empire (1500s)

British Empire

Big Question 2: Why is it important to study the British Empire?

The topic of the British Empire is one of the most fascinating and significant in the story of Britain. It is also deeply controversial, very divisive and totally relevant in today's world. So, what is it about the story of the British Empire that makes its study so important?

Objectives
- Examine reasons why the British Empire should be studied.

The British Empire helped shape the world we live in

Of the world's 203 nation states today, 63 were once ruled by Britain. About 20 others were briefly occupied by Britain. So, around a third of the world's nations experienced British rule or influence at one point or another. The British made an impact on these places, which experienced huge social, economic and political changes as a result. What the British Empire left behind is something that should be questioned, discussed, and debated.

The history of the British Empire helps us make sense of other things too. It helps us uncover answers to interesting questions – such as why English is spoken in so many countries, and why Britain is such a multicultural society.

▼ INTERPRETATION A Sathnam Sanghera, a British journalist and author, in an interview with *History Extra* magazine, 2021.

> 'The fundamental reason we are a multicultural society today is because we had an empire. That's a very basic point, but one that I think we nonetheless struggle to comprehend as a society. The reason that I, as a person of colour, am in this country is because Britons went over to India a few centuries ago.'

Later on... 2020

A 2020 YouGov survey of 1,684 British people found that 59 per cent felt that the British Empire was something to be proud of. Also, those surveyed tended to think Britain left its colonies better off – and a third would like it to still exist.

The British Empire is a window into the past

The Empire gives us an insight into how people used to live. For example, we can examine what life was like for the people who lived in places before the British invaded – and then see how the British changed this.

We can also explore the way people used to think. When the empire was being built, most people in Britain were proud of it – and generally believed that 'empire-building' was the right thing to do. Studying the British Empire allows us to explore why they thought this, and learn how these attitudes have changed.

The British Empire is relevant

The consequences of the empire are still felt widely and debated today. When the British took control of places, they often drew up new borders that split the local people into new countries and regions. In some areas, this caused huge problems at the time – and even today, these changes still cause conflict, particularly the way the British divided up India in 1947.

The way we remember the British Empire is a 'hot topic'. For example, there has been a debate in recent years about some of the statues of people connected to the empire in public places such as parks and town centres. Some people argue that some statues should be taken down because the actions, beliefs or views held by the figures when they were alive are no longer acceptable. Others argue the statues should stay because they teach us about the past, even if attitudes have changed and what they did is now seen as wrong.

Big Question

▶ **SOURCE B**

In June 2020, demonstrators in Bristol pulled down a statue of Edward Colston, a major trader in enslaved Africans, and threw it into the harbour. When he died in 1721, he left a lot of money to charities and good causes – and a statue of him was put up in 1895. Many people argue that it isn't right that he should be celebrated with a statue because he made his fortune through human suffering.

Key Words

multicultural

▼ **INTERPRETATION C**

An artist's impression of Hōne Heke and other Māori chopping down the British flagpole.

It is important to see a full picture

All schools try to make sure what they teach is challenging, thought-provoking and engaging. Studying the British Empire means that you can challenge the way you think about things. For example, most students will cover the causes and events of the First World War in History lessons. But it's just as important to cover the contribution of the British Empire to the outcome of the war. Soldiers from British colonies such as India, Nigeria, Kenya, Jamaica, Australia, Canada and South Africa fought and died fighting for the British. In fact, by autumn 1914 one in every three soldiers fighting for Britain in France was from India!

You can discover hidden stories

The British Empire made an impact all over the world over centuries. Exploring empire history allows us to learn some of the 'hidden' stories that might be unfamiliar to you – such as the Māori leader Hōne Heke who became so frustrated by the British in New Zealand that he cut down the flagpole that carried the UK flag (see page 71). And when the flagpole was rebuilt, he cut it down again. And then he did it again. And again. Or the clever military tactics of Zulu King Cetshwayo who outsmarted a large British army in southern Africa – and years later, when living in London, became a celebrity who met Queen Victoria and the prime minister.

Over to You

Imagine you've told someone at home (a parent, carer, or sibling, for example) that you've just started the topic of the British Empire at school. In response, they asked you, 'Why are you studying that?'

In full sentences, write down what you would say in response.

British Empire

Big Question 3: Why did Britain want an empire?

When a country extends its power, influence and control over other countries and areas of land, it is known as '**imperialism**'. Just like the word 'empire', it comes from the Roman word 'imperium', which was a type of legal title meaning that a person was in control, or had command over something. By the 1500s, two of the most powerful nations in Europe at this time were Spain and Portugal, both of which had overseas empires. Britain began to extend its power, influence and control over other countries at this time too. So, why did Britain want an empire? And how did it get it?

Objectives
- Examine why Britain wanted an empire.
- Explain how Britain got an empire.

Why did Britain want an empire?

The four main reasons why Britain wanted an empire were:
1. to get valuable raw materials and riches (such as diamonds, gold, spices, sugar and tea) that were found in other countries
2. so it could sell goods to the people in the colonies and make money
3. to become a more powerful country and strengthen their position in the world
4. because some people thought it was the right thing to do.

▼ **INTERPRETATION A** Written in 2019 by Peter Crowhurst, an author and retired History teacher.

'Land was now being annexed [invaded and taken over], not just for purposes of trade but to improve Britain's strategic position around the world and to prevent other powers from strengthening their own empires. It seemed that if you wanted to be a great power you had to have an empire.'

▼ **INTERPRETATION B** Adapted from a section titled 'Attitudes of Empire' on a BBC revision webpage about 'The British Empire through Time' (2019).

'Many goods were of interest to the Europeans, most specifically silk, calico, dyes, saltpeter [to preserve meat], cotton, pepper, cardamom, other spices and tea. India, the Europeans believed, would be easy to **exploit**.'

▼ **INTERPRETATION C** From a 2022 article on the National Geographic Kids website called 'British Empire Facts'.

'When the empire was being built, British people largely believed they were doing the right thing. In their eyes, they were improving and developing lands and bringing order to non-white countries which – due to racist attitudes – they thought were "uncivilised" and "backward". The British also believed they were doing the work of God by spreading Christianity – which they considered to be the "right" religion.'

▼ **INTERPRETATION D** From a History textbook written by Bea Stimpson, 2000.

'The colonies had to purchase all their manufactured goods from Britain. This gave Britain a guaranteed market for its manufacturers.'

How did Britain get its empire?

War

If Britain won a war against another country, it could often take over any land the other country controlled around the world. For example, when Britain won the Seven Years War (1756–1763) against France, land previously conquered by France in America and India became part of the British Empire. British victories in war were also how Canada and Caribbean islands such as Tobago and St Lucia became part of the empire. Little thought was given to the Indigenous peoples who had lived in Britain's so-called 'new' lands for centuries.

European exploration

The 1500s is often referred to as the 'Age of Discovery' in Europe. 'New' thinking about the world and better shipbuilding led to more exploration of land that Europeans had not visited before. Occasionally, explorers would find land and claim it for Britain. That happened in 1770 when Captain James Cook sailed to Australia. To strengthen the claim that the land belonged to Britain, British colonists who went there built towns. The people who already lived there – the Indigenous Australians – faced increasing threats to their land.

Settlers

Sometimes British people would go to another part of the world and start to live there. They might be looking for new business opportunities or a chance to own land, or be running away from the ill-treatment they received in their home country as a result of their religion. This is how large parts of the North American east coast became part of the British Empire in the 1600s and 1700s. Treaties were agreed between Indigenous peoples and the settlers, but over time the settlers often did not keep to these agreements and grabbed more and more land, leading to conflict.

Big Question

Key Words   imperialism   exploit

Trade

When British companies went to trade in some places, they slowly took over large areas. These companies sometimes became so powerful that they controlled the trade of luxury goods like spices, cotton, silk and tea. The British government sometimes sent and hired soldiers to support the companies by enforcing colonial order, guarding trading settlements and controlling the local people. This happened in India and parts of Africa for many years from the 1600s.

A long process?

As you can see, the British Empire developed in different ways. Sometimes it took over areas quickly, but often things took much longer. For example, the British first went to India to trade in the early 1600s, but India did not officially become part of the empire until Queen Victoria's reign in the mid-1800s.

Over to You

1. Define 'imperialism'.
2. Study **Interpretations A to D**.
   a. Can you match each one with the four reasons why Britain wanted an empire?
   b. In your own words, explain why Britain wanted an empire. You must use a quotation from each of **Interpretations A, B, C and D** in your answer.

Knowledge and Understanding

Describe two methods used by the British to gain an empire.

British Empire

1.1 What was North America like before the British arrived?

People lived in the Americas and Caribbean islands long before the arrival of the Europeans. Known as Indigenous peoples, they are the continents' original inhabitants. The first Indigenous American peoples probably travelled from Asia into what is now Alaska in North America. Some scientists believe this happened between about 15,000 and 20,000 years ago. Slowly, these peoples spread southwards, throughout North and South America and the Caribbean.

Objectives

- Describe how Indigenous nations were closely connected to their environment.
- Explain how we know about the history of Indigenous peoples.

Indigenous Americans

The Indigenous peoples of North America were generally grouped into **tribes** or nations, based on the region in which they lived and their shared customs, culture, languages and religion. There were hundreds of Indigenous nations throughout North America, speaking many different languages and dialects.

Sometimes large nations splintered into smaller communities, but as far as historians can understand, they largely lived in peace with each other. It has been estimated that the Indigenous population of North America was seven million to ten million in 1492, when the first European colonisers arrived.

▶ **MAP A** North America before the British arrived.

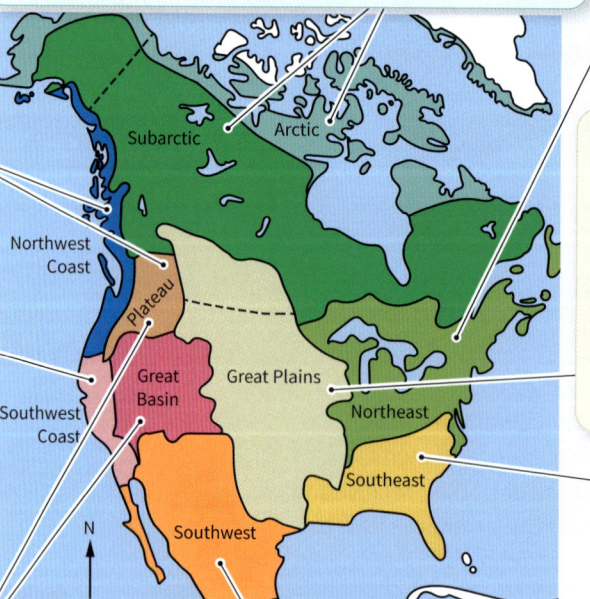

Arctic/Subarctic: groups such as the Eyak, Iñupiat and Yupik survived the cold, harsh environment by hunting whales, seals, wolves, rabbits and reindeer.

Northeast: the area was covered by forests, hills, mountains, lakes and streams. Groups such as the Iroquois fished and hunted deer, but they also farmed corn, beans and squash.

Northwest Coast/Plateau: the ocean and coastal forests provided peoples such as the Tlingit, Chinook and Coast Salish with all they needed. They hunted otters, seals and whales in long canoes that could fit up to 30 people, and were known for their large houses, made of cedar planks, and their **totem poles**.

Great Plains: groups such as the Apsáalooke, the Comanche and the Kiowa were **nomadic** people who moved, constantly following the great **bison** herds that fed on the grassland. The bison were hunted for meat, but also provided materials for making shelter, tools and clothing.

Southwest Coast: the variety of habitats (forests, mountains, coastline, etc.) meant that hundreds of smaller groups developed lifestyles suited to the environment. Nations such as the Tolowa and Cahto lived in forest areas, while the Chumash lived on the coast.

Southeast: among the Southeast tribes were the Biloxi, Chickasaw and Cherokee. They tended to stay in one place and were skilled farmers. The climate was warm and the land was fertile. Common farming crops were corn, beans and squash. They hunted deer, beavers, squirrels, rabbits – even alligators (in what is now Florida).

Great Basin/Plateau: the mountains, rivers, deserts, forests and large areas of flat grassland (called 'plains') provided all that was needed by the hundreds of nations in these regions. Some groups in particular (such as the Ute and Nimíipuu) were known as expert horse breeders, riders and traders. Horses arrived with the Spanish, who had colonised some parts of North America in the early 1500s.

Southwest: a dry region with little rainfall. As a result, the Indigenous communities had to be creative when planting crops to take advantage of any water in the area. Most peoples of the Southwest combined farming with hunting and gathering. Nations included the Apache, Navajo and Mojave. The Pueblo people, for example, lived in tiered homes made out of stone and clay adobe bricks.

14   Chapter 1: British America

Contact with Europeans

As far as Europeans were concerned, before the late 1400s their known world consisted of the continents of Europe, Africa and Asia. They did not know that the Americas (the continents of North and South America) and the islands of the Caribbean existed. However, all that changed in 1492 when Christopher Columbus accidentally sailed to the Caribbean (he thought he was on his way to China or India). In the years that followed, many European countries claimed ownership of land in the Caribbean and the Americas. Over time, the British began to build up colonies on the east coast of North America, adding much more territory following a war against France.

In general, the relationship between the Indigenous peoples and Europeans started quite peacefully. Trading was common. For example, Europeans might offer textiles, glass beads, mirrors and metal products in exchange for food, animal skins and furs. Gradually, however, wars between European colonisers started to involve Indigenous nations who allied themselves to one side of the war or another. Europeans also brought diseases with them to which the Indigenous people had no resistance as they had never encountered them before. These diseases killed millions and resulted in a huge decline in population.

▼ **SOURCE B** Taos, an Indigenous American village in New Mexico, USA. The village has existed since around 1000CE and is the oldest continuously inhabited place in the US.

How do we know about the history of Indigenous peoples?

Indigenous Americans passed on their history and culture through a rich tradition of storytelling, which we can still learn from today (known as **oral history**). We can also learn from ceremonies and traditions that have been passed down the generations.

Key Words

tribe   totem pole   nomadic   bison   oral history

Some Indigenous nations used pictograms to record important events. Other artefacts such as textiles, tools, weapons and pottery, provide evidence about how Indigenous peoples lived in the past.

We can also build up a basic picture from the recordings (letters, diaries, drawings) of the Europeans who colonised or visited North America. However, we must remember that the information they record is based on their own views of people they did not fully understand.

▼ **INTERPRETATION C** A Comanche settlement of teepees, with women drying meat and preparing bison skins. From an 1841 book by George Catlin, a white American traveller.

Over to You

1. Who were the original inhabitants of the Americas and the Caribbean?
2. What was the estimated Indigenous population of North America at the time of the first European expeditions?
3. a Make a list of the key areas or regions where Indigenous peoples of North America lived.
   b For each area/region, write down one fact or piece of information.

Similarity and Difference

How do we know about the history of Indigenous Americans? In what ways is it similar to, and different from, how we know about the history of Britain?

British Empire 15

1.2A How did the British Empire begin?

It is hard to pin down when, exactly, the British Empire began. However, some historians put the date at 5 March 1496, when King Henry VII (Henry VIII's father) asked an Italian explorer to go out and search for any 'islands, countries, regions or provinces' that were 'unknown to all Christians'. If the explorer found any lands that other European nations had not been to, he was to claim them for England. Many people pinpoint this request as the start of the British Empire. So, why did King Henry VII ask the explorer to set sail? Where did he sail to? And what exactly did he find?

> **Objectives**
> - Explain how the British Empire began in North America.
> - Describe the role of key individuals in the early growth of the British Empire.
> - Contrast different viewpoints on Christopher Columbus.

An age of discovery

In the late 1400s, Europeans were finding out more and more about the world. Across Europe, writers, sculptors, doctors, mathematicians, scientists, painters and designers began to ask questions about their current methods and experiment with new ideas. This period in history is often called the **Renaissance**, which is a French word for 'rebirth'.

Spain and Portugal

The Renaissance wasn't only a time when Europeans were curious to know how the world worked – they were also keen to take over parts of the world *outside* Europe. In the late 1400s, Spain and Portugal were two of the most powerful countries in Europe – and they both began to set up large empires. Their monarchs were keen to find land that other Europeans had not found, and Portuguese and Spanish merchants were eager to expand their businesses and find new sea routes to India, China and Indonesia. In 1487, Portuguese ships became the first in Europe to get round the bottom of the African continent. This opened up a sea route to the East – and the Portuguese made a fortune from selling goods brought from abroad to wealthy Europeans.

The Americas

Spain soon followed Portugal, and in 1492 Spanish ships under the guidance of Christopher Columbus (an Italian working for Spain) set out for China and India but headed in the opposite direction – westwards. Columbus knew that the world was a sphere and thought that to get to the East it was possible to sail west over the sea until you reached China and Indonesia. Remember, Europeans had absolutely no idea that the continents of North and South America existed, so they did not realise they would reach these areas first.

After reaching this unexpected land, Columbus claimed ownership of much of South America and the Caribbean for Spain, though he did not immediately colonise it. Soon Portugal claimed Brazil. But neither Spain nor Portugal landed in North America (what we now call the USA and Canada).

▶ **SOURCE A** This map, by Henricus Martellus from around 1489, shows what Europeans thought the world was like at that time.

Chapter 1: British America

▼ **MAP B** Columbus thought he could sail all the way to Asia. He had no idea the huge continents of North and South America were in between.

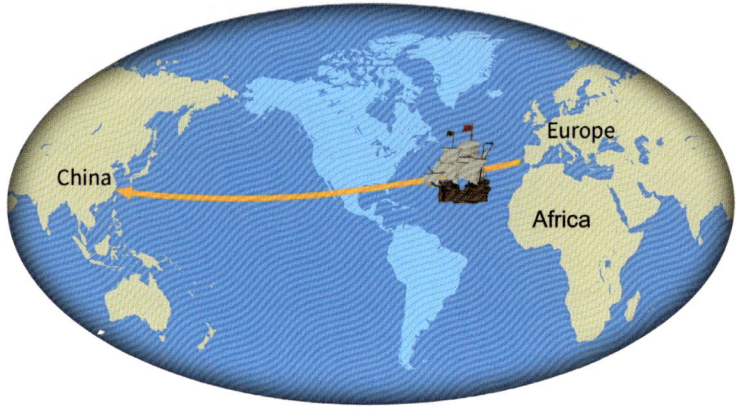

Here comes Henry

In 1496, England joined the 'age of exploration', when King Henry VII gave an Italian explorer called John Cabot the task of finding new lands for England (see **Source C**). In 1497, Cabot sailed westwards from Bristol across the Atlantic Ocean. A few months later, he landed on the coast of what the King called the 'New Found Launde', in what we now call Canada.

However, there were no silks, spices or gold to be found there, so Cabot came home. But this brief visit was the start of English monarchs claiming parts of America for themselves and the nation. Over time, British people would colonise Canada – and more would follow, colonising land all along the eastern coastline of what became the USA. The age of British people taking land and living in overseas colonies had arrived.

▼ **SOURCE C** Orders given to John Cabot by Henry VII, March 1496. Note that the orders use the terms 'heathen' and 'infidel' to describe non-Christians. These insulting terms are used to describe a person who has no religion or whose religion is not that of the person using the insult.

> 'You have full and free authority to sail to all parts and countries of the East, West and North under our banners and ensigns [flags] with five ships and as many sailors as they can hold, to seek out, discover and find whatever islands, countries, regions or provinces of the heathen and infidels whosoever they be, and in what part of the world they be, which before this time have been unknown to all Christians.'

Key Words

▶ **SOURCE D** This vandalised statue of Christopher Columbus is in London's Belgrave Square. In recent years, there have been calls for statues of Columbus to be removed because of his colonial links. In the USA, at least 36 monuments to Columbus have been removed since the 1970s – but he is still the third most commemorated figure in the country.

Later on... TODAY

During his lifetime, Columbus was seen as a hero to many people. For centuries, statues have been created to commemorate his voyages. Today, many people view him differently. Some see him as a lucky explorer who landed in the Americas by chance, rather than skill. Others point to the fact that he enslaved many Indigenous people when he returned to the Caribbean – and began an era of conquest in which European colonisers stole land and natural resources in the Americas.

Over to You

1. Can you think of two reasons why people at this time were keen to find new lands?
2. a Look at **Source A**. Describe the source – what does it show?
   b Which major continents were unknown to Europeans at the time this map was drawn?
3. How were Columbus, King Henry VII and Cabot important in the early years of the British Empire?

Cause and Consequence

Explain why some statues of Columbus have been removed or defaced.

British Empire

1.2B How did the British Empire begin?

A false start?

No English colonisers went to live in Newfoundland. Cabot returned home and the Indigenous peoples continued to live their lives as before. Over the next few years Spanish, Portuguese, French and English fishermen went to catch cod in the area, but no Europeans actually stayed.

In fact, the kings and queens who immediately followed Henry VII (his son Henry VIII and then Edward VI and Mary I) did little to expand England's territory overseas. Instead, they encouraged sailors and merchants to find new trade routes to China, India and the Maluku Islands (then known as the Spice Islands). But all this changed when Elizabeth I (Henry VII's granddaughter) became queen.

A new era

A period of exploration began during Queen Elizabeth's reign (1558–1603). To begin with, Elizabeth encouraged sailors to launch attacks on Spanish and Portuguese ships to steal gold, silver, jewels and silk. Later, in the 1570s and 1580s, she asked them to go out and claim new lands for England and make valuable trading contacts in these lands. Soon English people began to colonise and live in these places.

Humphrey Gilbert

In 1578, Elizabeth gave permission to an explorer named Humphrey Gilbert to travel to North America and build a colony. The colonisers hoped to farm, fish and perhaps find gold. However, Gilbert's ships were scattered by storms in the Atlantic Ocean and never reached North America. In 1583, Gilbert tried again. After landing in North America, he claimed hundreds of miles of land for the Queen.

> ▶ **SOURCE E** A portrait of Queen Elizabeth I painted to commemorate England's defeat of the Spanish Navy (or Armada) in 1588. In the background to the right you can see stormy weather and lots of wrecked Spanish ships. To the left you can see English ships sailing in the sunshine. The crown next to Elizabeth is called the 'Imperial Crown', which means a crown for emperors, who rule over empires. Note the globe in the painting – the Queen is pointing to the newly 'found' continent of the Americas, and particularly a region in North America – Virginia!

But Gilbert made no attempt to form a colony because he lacked food and supplies, so he set off back to England – although his ship sank and he drowned. Today, however, the area around where Gilbert landed is regarded as one of the first parts of the British Empire.

> **Fact** ✓
>
> When Christopher Columbus arrived in America he called the Indigenous people 'Indians' because he believed he had reached India. Today, the Indigenous peoples of North America are often called American Indians or Native Americans (in the USA) and First Nations (in Canada).

'New World' colonisers

In 1584, Queen Elizabeth asked another explorer, Walter Raleigh, to create colonies in North America. In 1584, 1585 and 1587, Raleigh organised voyages to North America and land was claimed around Roanoke Island (now in North Carolina). It was named 'Virginia' in honour of Queen Elizabeth, who was known as the Virgin Queen. These early colonies failed, and no English colonisers stayed there, but in 1607, when King James I was on the throne, a group of colonisers did manage to permanently settle and start new lives out in what they called the 'New World'. By James' death in 1625, English women and men lived in colonies in Virginia, Bermuda, Newfoundland, and New England. They built homes and grew crops like tobacco, sugar and cotton, which they sold to Britain, making lots of money.

Impact of British colonisers on Indigenous Americans

Millions of Indigenous peoples lived in North America long before Europeans invaded to claim lands and take resources from the continent and its inhabitants. There were many nations, often with strong links between them. For example, the British colonists in Virginia were in the territory of the powerful Powhatans who were keen to trade with the British for their guns and other manufactured products. For many years the British colonists struggled to survive. At the same time the diseases they carried with them caused thousands of Indigenous deaths due to their lack of disease resistance. During this early period of colonisation, the British knew almost nothing about the rest of America, and had very little impact on the majority of Indigenous Americans.

▼ **SOURCE F** An illustration from 1590 showing English colonisers approaching the island of Roanoke in 1585. It accompanied a report that tried to persuade others that there should be more British colonisation in North America.

Fact ✓

On 18 August 1587, a woman named Eleanor Dare gave birth to the first child of English parents born in North America. She was named Virginia.

Later on...  1914–1918

During the First World War, Indigenous Americans who were fluent in both their traditional language and English were used by the US army to send secret messages in battle. They became known as 'code talkers'.

Over to You

1 Each of these dates is important in the early years of Britain's empire:

   1607; 1587; 1584; 1496; 1578; 1583

   Write the dates in order. Beside each date, write what happened in that year.

2 Look at **Source E**.
   a Describe the image.
   b What role did this person play in the early years of the British Empire?
   c In this period, kings and queens wanted to create a certain impression with their portraits. What impression does this portrait try to create of Queen Elizabeth? Pick two details and explain the impression they give.

   NOTE: An important way that historians use sources is through inference: historians 'read between the lines' to work out what sources might be suggesting, rather than what is actually written or shown.

British Empire 19

1.3A Life in the colonies

In the sixteenth and early seventeenth centuries, people began to leave European countries such as Spain, France, Britain, the Netherlands, Sweden and Finland and settle in North America. Early British colonists occupied the east coast of North America. These British colonies made up what could be described as Britain's first large overseas empire. But who were the early colonists? Why did they leave Britain? What were the consequences of British colonisation for the Indigenous peoples of America?

Objectives

- Outline where European colonies were established in North America.
- Identify how Britain came to dominate the continent.
- Explain the impact of colonisation on Indigenous peoples.

Jamestown, 1607

In the late 1500s, many British people had tried to establish colonies in the area known as Virginia, but they failed to survive. In 1606, King James I gave permission for a group of business people to sail to Virginia, to establish a new colony called Jamestown, to see if the land was fit to grow crops, and to find gold if possible. The colony was founded in 1607.

There was some conflict between the early colonists and the Indigenous Algonquian peoples in the area whose land they were trying to colonise. However, the colonists had to rely on local Indigenous people to help them find and grow food – particularly as some of the early colonists were wealthy aristocrats who were not used to farming.

Life in Jamestown meant hunger and death for many, but the colonists were determined to stay. With the help of some Indigenous people, the colonists began to farm the land, rather than focus on the search for gold. Tobacco planting in particular led to the success of Jamestown: tobacco was easy to grow and made high profits. This led to more British migrants seeking their fortune in what they termed the 'New World'.

Meanwhile...  1756–1763

Conflict took place in many areas of the world where the European countries involved controlled land, such as in the Caribbean, Africa and India. For these reasons, some historians have called the Seven Years War the 'first world war'.

Why did people leave Britain?

There were several reasons:

- Some left because they couldn't find well-paid work in Britain, and people struggled to survive. They sometimes faced starvation because of failed harvests. As a result, a new start in a new place seemed very appealing.
- Some Christian groups, such as Puritans, Quakers and Catholics, were not treated well in Britain. People from these religious groups left to settle in North America, where they could worship freely.
- People from overcrowded British towns were excited by the vast expanse of land in America, and by the chance to make money. Settlers grew crops such as tobacco, sugar, corn and cotton, and then transported these back to Britain to sell.

Taking more land

After the establishment of Jamestown, the British continued to take lots of land, stretching over 1,600km, along the east coast of North America. The colonists split themselves up into separate areas, or colonies, and farmed the land – growing cotton, tobacco, corn, oats, potatoes, wheat and barley. Other countries took land too. The French occupied land in the northern part of North America (now Canada) and inland around the Mississippi and St Lawrence rivers. Both the French and the British were well armed, and built forts to guard their land. The Spanish had colonised land in North America too, in the south of the continent. Of course, much of this land was already inhabited before the colonists arrived.

▼ **MAP A** A map showing how land in North America was divided up by European settlers in the 1600s and early 1700s.

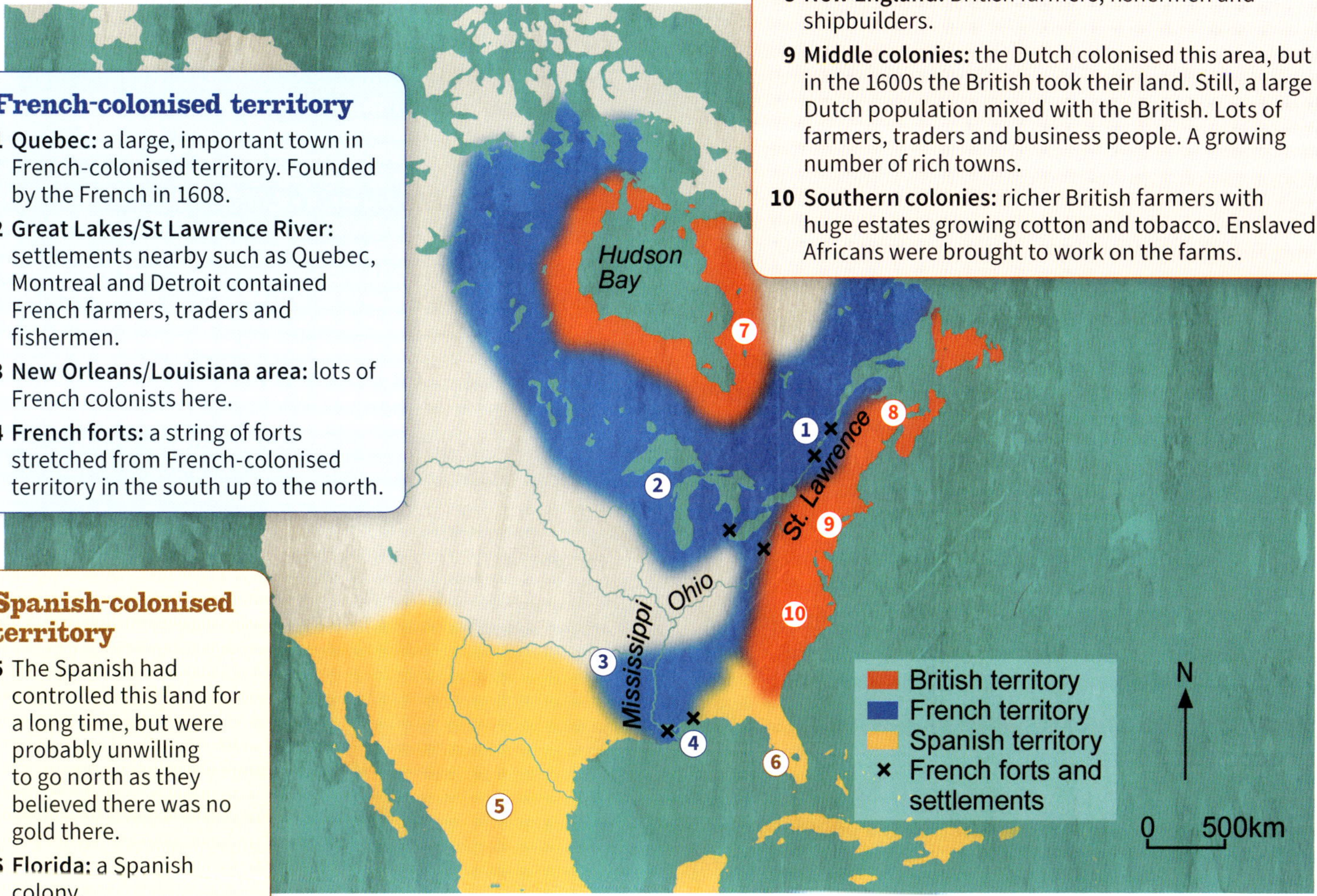

French-colonised territory

1 **Quebec:** a large, important town in French-colonised territory. Founded by the French in 1608.
2 **Great Lakes/St Lawrence River:** settlements nearby such as Quebec, Montreal and Detroit contained French farmers, traders and fishermen.
3 **New Orleans/Louisiana area:** lots of French colonists here.
4 **French forts:** a string of forts stretched from French-colonised territory in the south up to the north.

Spanish-colonised territory

5 The Spanish had controlled this land for a long time, but were probably unwilling to go north as they believed there was no gold there.
6 **Florida:** a Spanish colony.

British-colonised territory

7 **Hudson Bay:** a few hundred British hunters lived in this area.
8 **New England:** British farmers, fishermen and shipbuilders.
9 **Middle colonies:** the Dutch colonised this area, but in the 1600s the British took their land. Still, a large Dutch population mixed with the British. Lots of farmers, traders and business people. A growing number of rich towns.
10 **Southern colonies:** richer British farmers with huge estates growing cotton and tobacco. Enslaved Africans were brought to work on the farms.

The Seven Years War

By the mid-1700s, Britain and France had the largest European presence in North America, but there was tension between the two countries. The French wanted the rich land that the British had colonised and farmed near the east coast, and the British wanted to expand into French-colonised land so they could set up more farms. Between 1756 and 1763, these two European nations fought each other for total control of North America.

The Seven Years War wasn't just a conflict between Britain and France – other countries took sides. For example, Britain was supported by the states of Prussia and Hanover (now in modern-day Germany) while France had help from Austria, Russia and Sweden. Spain (with France) and Portugal (with Britain) were later drawn into the conflict too. After years of bitter and bloody fighting, in which both sides were helped by Indigenous soldiers, Britain won the war and took control of most of France's territory in North America, including Canada. Now Britain was the dominant European nation in North America.

Over to You

1 Look at **Map A**. In your own words, describe how different European countries had divided up parts of North America between themselves.

2 a Write down three facts about the Seven Years War.
  b Why do some people refer to the Seven Years War as the 'first world war'?

Cause

Describe two reasons why people from European nations wanted to colonise North America.

British Empire

1.3B Life in the colonies

How did the colonists get the land?

When the European colonists went to the Americas, Indigenous peoples were already living there. There was conflict – many Indigenous nations, such as the Iroquois, saw the settlers as invaders, while the colonists believed they were superior to the Indigenous peoples, and felt they had a right to live wherever they wanted (see **Interpretation B**). In the British-controlled areas of North America, for example, the colonists usually drove local Indigenous communities away and destroyed the forests so they could farm the land themselves. Massacres were carried out on both sides over land claims, but some colonists were particularly vicious: they often attacked and destroyed Indigenous peoples' crops and villages. They also took Indigenous children away from their families, to be forcibly taught English ways of life.

Long-term impact

In 1500, there were approximately 560,000 Indigenous Americans in territories colonised by the British. However, by 1700, there were fewer than 280,000. Devastating European diseases such as measles and smallpox, the ill treatment of Indigenous American peoples, and British expansion into Indigenous territory all had a huge impact. Many Indigenous peoples had to find a new way of life, were forced to adapt to European ways, or had to move further inland to avoid the colonists. Some Indigenous nations negotiated trade deals and treaties with the colonisers that guaranteed some protections from European settlers, but today, Indigenous Americans account for under one per cent of the total population of the USA. In spite of this, there are about 574 different nation groups recognised by the United States government who have retained their culture and customs in spite of attempts to destroy their ways of living.

▶ **SOURCE B** The Grand Union Flag. This is seen by many as the USA's first flag. The 13 stripes represent the 13 colonies, while the Union Flag indicates the tie to the UK.

Later on...

According to recent reports, there are approximately 2.5 million Indigenous people in the USA (out of a population of 336 million) and around one million in Canada (out of a population of 39 million).

▼ **INTERPRETATION C** Adapted from an article called 'The making of a nation – American history' on an educational website, written in 2012 by Steve Ember, an author and broadcaster.

'Perhaps the most serious was the difference in the way that the American Indians [Indigenous Americans] and the Europeans thought about land. This difference created problems that would not be solved during the next several hundred years.

Owning land was extremely important to the European settlers. Land meant wealth and power. Many of the settlers who came to North America could never have owned land back home in Europe. They were too poor. When they arrived in the 'new world', they discovered that no one seemed to own the huge amounts of land. For many, it was a dream come true.

On the other hand, the American Indians believed that no one could own land. They believed, however, that anyone could use it to live on and grow crops. They might hunt on one area of land for some time, but then they would move on. They hunted only what they could eat, so populations of animals could continue to increase. They did not understand that the settlers were going to keep the land. To them, it was like trying to own the air, or the clouds. As the years passed, more settlers arrived, and took more land. They cut down trees. They built fences to keep people and animals out. They demanded that the American Indians stay off their land.'

▼ **SOURCE D** Chief Powhatan, leader of the Powhatan chiefdom of Indigenous Americans, said the following to the coloniser Captain John Smith in the early 1600s:

'Your coming is not for trade, but to invade my people and possess my country.'

▼ **MAP E** The 13 American colonies, the goods and crops they produced, and early British settlements.

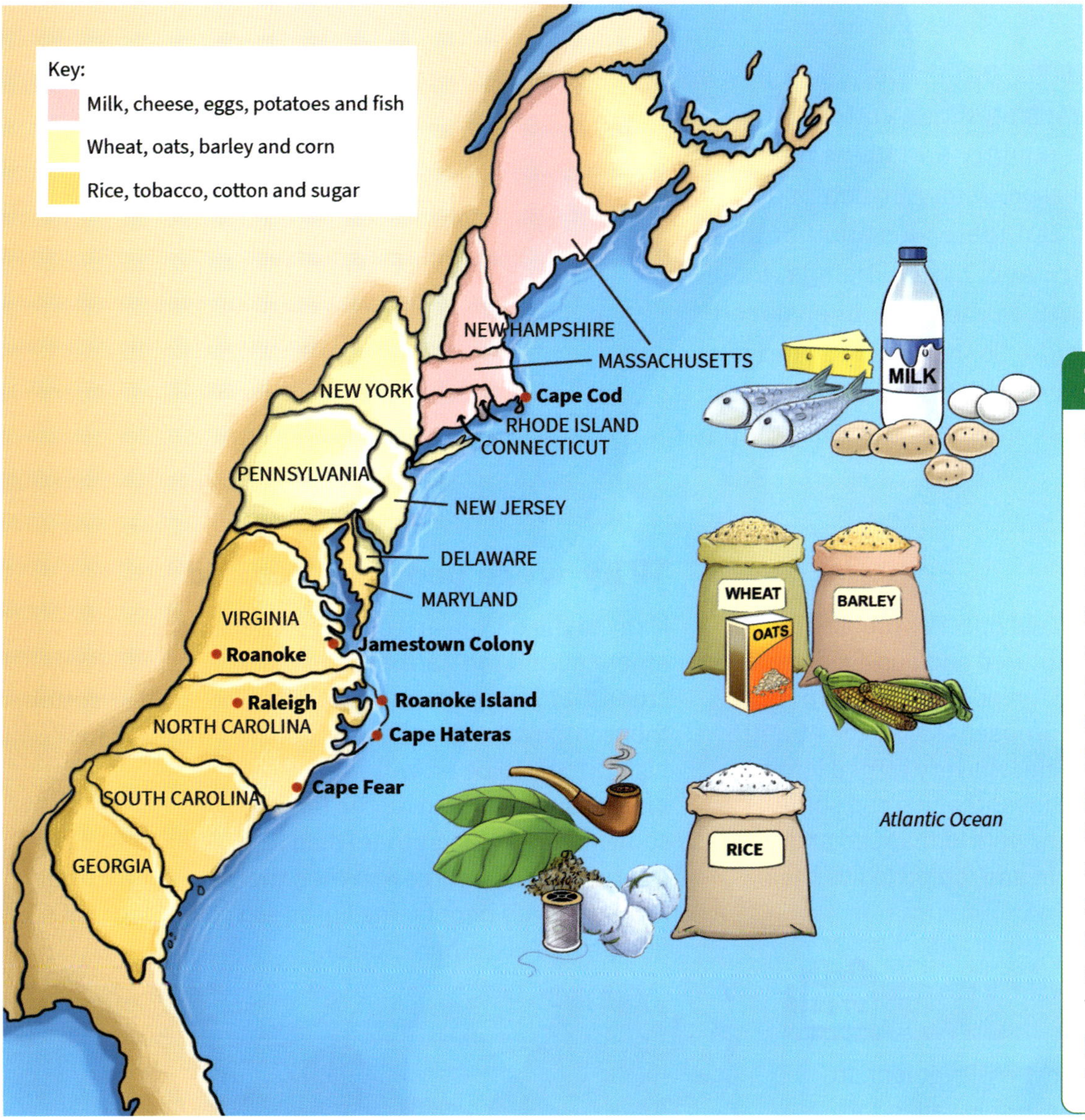

Key:
- Milk, cheese, eggs, potatoes and fish
- Wheat, oats, barley and corn
- Rice, tobacco, cotton and sugar

Fact

One of the best-known groups of British people to colonise North America arrived in 1620 on a ship called the *Mayflower*. They were mainly Puritans (strict Protestant Christians) who left because they were persecuted for their religious beliefs. They, and other colonists, set up their own religious colony known as 'New Plymouth'. These colonists became known as the 'Pilgrim Fathers'.

Over to You

1 Look at **Source B**.
   a Draw the flag in your book.
   b Label your flag with its name. Underneath it, write an explanation of what the stripes represented. Why was the Union Flag included?
2 a Describe the impact of British colonisation for the Indigenous peoples of America.
   b What was the British attitude to Indigenous American peoples in the sixteenth and seventeenth centuries? Explain your answer.

Source Analysis

1 Study **Interpretation C**. According to this interpretation, what differences were there between the way Europeans and Indigenous Americans viewed land ownership?
2 How could you follow up **Interpretation C** to find out more about the conflict between Indigenous Americans and European settlers? Write down:
   a A detail you would follow up
   b A question you would ask
   c What type of source you could use
   d How this might help answer your question

British Empire

1.4A Britain and the trade in enslaved Africans

During the 1500s and 1600s, Britain became a powerful trading nation. Goods such as sugar, cotton and tobacco flooded into the country and items made in Britain were shipped abroad. Many British people became rich as a result. But there was another kind of trade happening – the trade in human beings, mainly from Africa. This is known as the trade in enslaved Africans, or the slave trade. So, how exactly did the trade in enslaved Africans work? How, and why, did it start? And how does this relate to the British Empire?

Objectives

- Outline the development of the trade in enslaved Africans in the sixteenth and seventeenth centuries.
- Describe the ways Britain was involved in the trade in enslaved Africans.
- Explain why the trade was so profitable.

Slavery

The idea of slavery is a very old one. For thousands of years, people have been captured and enslaved, treated as someone's property and forced to work. From around 1500 onwards, as Europeans sailed the Atlantic to trade and establish colonies, slavery turned into a profitable international business that earned some people millions, while others were kidnapped and taken to the other side of the world and forced to live their lives as enslaved people.

Why were people enslaved?

Many of the European colonists who moved to the Americas and the Caribbean were farmers who grew crops that were very popular in Europe, such as cotton, tobacco, sugar and coffee – and they sold them for high prices. To begin with, some farmers forced local Indigenous people to do the farming for them, but some ran away, and others died from disease or cruel treatment (see **Source A**). When there were not enough local enslaved people, the European colonists went to find people elsewhere: Africa.

Later on... 1742

Africans took action against enslavement. In 1742, in Sierra Leone, a slave ship called the *Jolly Batchelor* was attacked by Africans from the shore. The crew was killed and all the enslaved people on board were freed. There were more than 500 reported revolts aboard slave ships at sea too.

▶ **SOURCE A** An image from 1590 showing Spanish colonists slaughtering or capturing and enslaving Indigenous people in South America. At this time, the Spanish built a huge empire in South, Central and the southern part of North America. The trade in enslaved people was a key feature of this empire, as the Spanish needed Indigenous peoples to work in their silver mines and **plantations**.

▼ **MAP B** The three parts of the slave triangle.

Key Words plantation

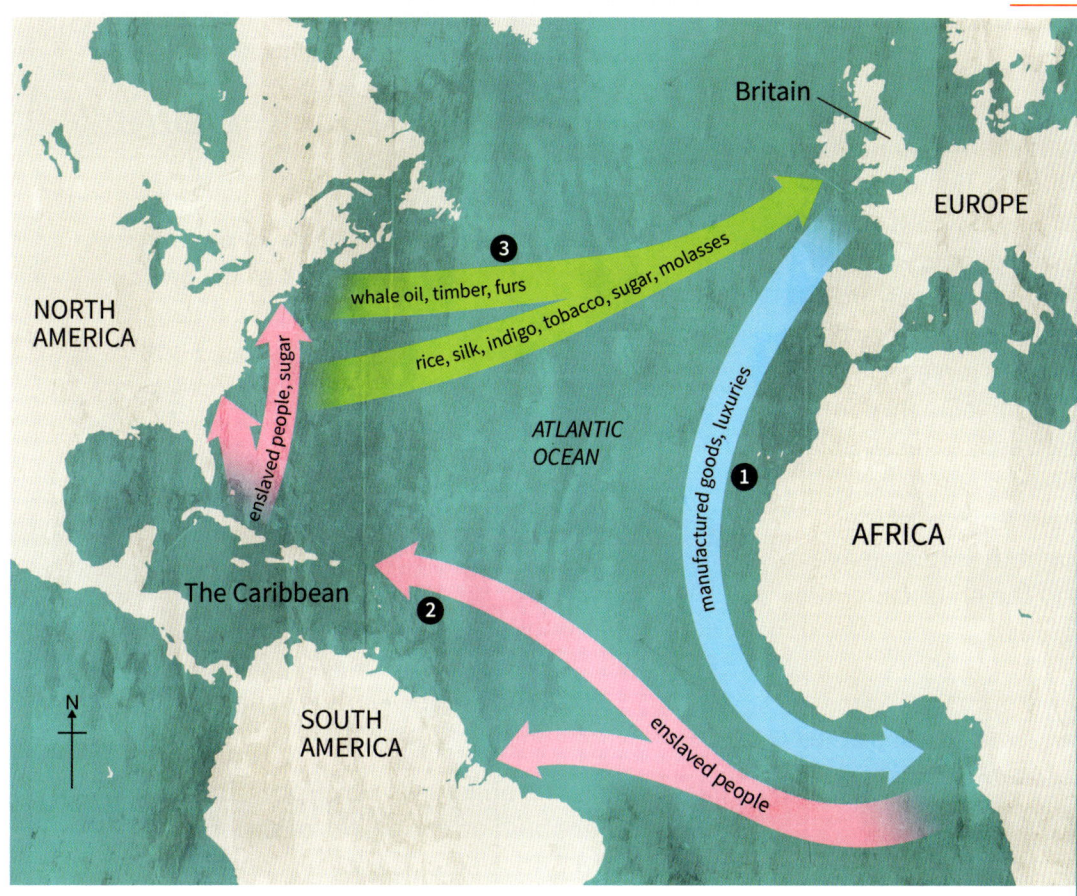

1. Traders leave Britain and other European ports, heading for Africa, with goods such as alcohol, guns and cloth.

2. Traders trade these goods with Africans in return for prisoners from other chiefdoms or kingdoms, who have been captured to sell; traders also kidnap Africans. Ships, loaded with enslaved Africans, sail across the Atlantic.

3. In the Americas, the enslaved Africans are traded to plantation owners and farmers for goods such as sugar, cotton or tobacco. Some are sold for money. The goods are shipped back to British or European ports to be sold at a large profit.

A 'slave triangle'

Enslaved Africans were forcibly taken to the Americas and the Caribbean as a result of a three-part trading journey known as the 'slave triangle'. Traders made money from all parts of the triangle, earning up to 800 per cent profit. They just needed the initial investment to pay for the ship, a strong crew to control the enslaved people, and goods to trade for enslaved people on the African coast.

Slave owners also profited: they forced enslaved people to work all their lives, without wages, and suffering terrible hardship.

When, exactly, did the British get involved?

British traders first got involved in the slave trade in 1562. That year, John Hawkins became England's first slave trader when he captured 300 people from Sierra Leone on the west coast of Africa and sold them in the Caribbean. He repeated the journey many times – and other slave traders copied him.

Over to You

1. Define the following:
   a enslaved person
   b trade in enslaved Africans or 'slave trade'

2. Describe how the trade in enslaved Africans developed in the sixteenth and seventeenth centuries.

3. a The trade in enslaved Africans is often referred to as 'triangular trade' or the 'slave triangle'. Why do you think it got these names?
   b Write a clear and organised summary that shows how and why the 'slave triangle' operated.

Knowledge and Understanding

Explain why the trade in enslaved Africans was so profitable for slave traders and owners.

British Empire

1.4B Britain and the trade in enslaved Africans

Enslaved people on British farms in the Americas and the Caribbean

While British people traded in enslaved people from the 1560s, historians know there were enslaved Africans working on British plantations (large farms) in Bermuda from at least 1616, and believe that the first enslaved people to work on British plantations in North America arrived from Africa in 1619. Enslaved people endured short and brutal lives of extreme misery: those on sugar plantations had an average life expectancy of 26, because the living conditions often forced them to have a poor diet, they faced tough punishments and had no proper medical attention. Despite the terrible conditions, enslaved Africans showed incredible resilience and held on to important aspects of their cultures. For example, they brought their knowledge of farming methods from Africa to the Americas and influenced the way crops were grown.

▼ **SOURCE C** Written by Harriet Ann Jacobs in her autobiography *Incidents in the Life of a Slave Girl* (1861). Jacobs was an African-American writer who escaped from slavery.

'I saw a mother lead seven children to the auction block. She knew that some of them would be taken from her; but they took all. The children were sold to a slave trader, and the mother was bought by a man in her own town. Before night, her children were all far away. She begged the trader to tell her where he intended to take them; this he refused to do. How could he when he knew he would sell them, one by one, wherever he could command the highest price? I met that mother in the street and her wild, haggard face lives today in my mind. She wrung her hands in anguish and exclaimed, "Gone, all gone! Why don't God kill me?"'

A royal connection

Britain wasn't the only European nation to get involved in slavery, but it made some of the largest profits. All sorts of people were involved. Queen Elizabeth I, for example, was a business partner of John Hawkins. King Charles II was a partner in the Royal African Company, a slave-trading business that transported 60,000 enslaved Africans between 1680 and 1688.

▼ **SOURCE D** Adapted from a 1784 book by James Ramsay, a British doctor working on the British-controlled Caribbean island of St Kitts. He was so shocked by the way enslaved people were treated that he wrote a book that inspired many anti-slavery campaigners.

'The ordinary punishments of slaves are whipping, beating with a stick – sometimes to the breaking of bones – chains, an iron ring around the neck or ankle, or being placed in a dungeon. There have been instances of slitting of ears, breaking of limbs, amputation, and taking out of eyes.'

Slave trade profits

The British trade in enslaved Africans, between the early 1600s and 1807, generated profits of about £12 million (over £1 billion today). This money helped to make Britain one of the world's richest and most powerful nations.

Many of the fine buildings in Liverpool, Bristol and London were built on the profits of slavery. In 1785, a well-known British actor George F. Cooke said, 'Every brick in the city of Liverpool is cemented with the blood of a slave.' In fact, 20 of Liverpool's mayors between 1787 and 1807 are thought to have been slave traders.

Indeed, many British people played a part in the slave trade – ship owners (who allowed their ships to be used), bankers (who lent them the money), investors (who shared in the profits) and importers (who brought in the goods that enslaved people produced).

▼ **TABLE E** The number of voyages to Africa, between 1695 and 1807, from some of the main European ports involved in the trade in enslaved Africans.

Port	Number of voyages to Africa (1695–1807)
Liverpool	5,300
London	3,100
Bristol	2,200
Other European ports (e.g. Lisbon and Barcelona)	450

▶ **SOURCE F** Liverpool Town Hall dates from 1749. According to historian David Richardson, at this time Liverpool was 'the undisputed slaving capital of England and by far the largest slave port in the Atlantic world'. The building has decorative carvings showing faces of African people, elephants, crocodiles and lions – references to the trade in enslaved Africans from which Liverpool gained lots of its wealth.

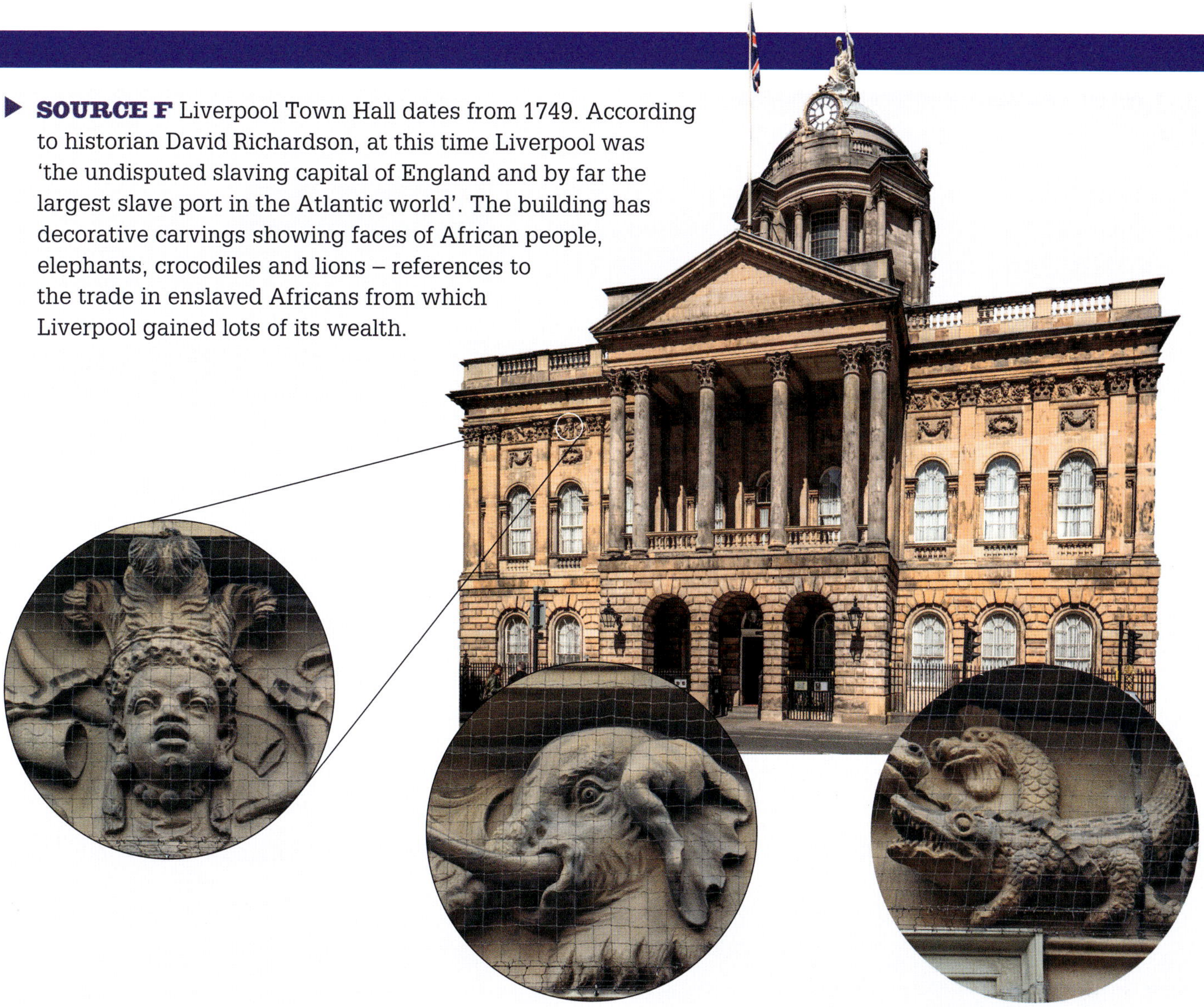

▼ **INTERPRETATION G** Adapted from an article by the journalist Mary Murtagh in the newspaper *The Liverpool Echo* in 2007.

'Evidence of Liverpool's slave trade past is all over the city – in its architecture, public buildings and street names… The city thrived doing ship repairs and importing goods with approximately half of Liverpool's trade linked to slavery. The movers and shakers among slave traders were immortalised with streets named after them.'

Over to You

1 Look at **Table E** and **Interpretation G**.
   a In what way was the city of Liverpool linked to the trade in enslaved Africans?
   b How did the people of Liverpool make money from the slave trade at the time?
   c Look through the text to find the quote from George F. Cooke. What do you think he meant?

Fact ✓

Portugal and Britain were the two most active slave-trading countries. It is estimated that between them they accounted for about 70 per cent of all Africans transported to the Americas and Caribbean.

Knowledge and Understanding

Write an account of how Britain was linked to the trade in enslaved Africans. You could include links through the royal family, British cities, traders or bankers, for example.

British Empire

1.5 Revolution

By the 1760s, the British had built an overseas empire in North America. They controlled a huge area of land on the eastern coast, stretching back from the Atlantic Ocean to the Mississippi River. This area was divided into 13 colonies, and each had strong ties to Britain. But in 1776, these 13 colonies broke away from Britain and declared themselves to be united as one independent country – the United States of America. How and why did this happen?

Objectives

- Describe how American colonies became independent from Britain.
- Explain why American colonists wanted independence from Britain.

Unsettled colonists

The people who lived in the British colonies of North America were tough and independently minded. Many of them were descended from religious groups who had gone to America to escape religious persecution, or because they were unhappy with the British monarch. The 13 colonies successfully traded with each other, and large profits were made. The trade in enslaved people also made vast sums of money. This led to many colonists feeling that they could exist separately from Britain. Some felt no connection to Britain either – they had been born in America and regarded themselves as 'Americans'.

Unfair rules

The American colonists were particularly upset about the following:

- The colonists had to sell key money-making goods, such as cotton, tobacco and sugar, directly to Britain and nowhere else. This effectively prevented the colonies from trading with other countries.
- If the colonists wanted to buy anything from other countries, the goods had to go to Britain first – where they were *taxed*. Before long, colonists were paying taxes on paint, glass, wine, newspapers – even playing cards and dice!

I want to break free

As resentment grew in America about the taxes paid to the British government, tension began to build. The colonists were especially upset when the British government taxed their cups of tea – three pence to Britain for every pound of tea sold in America. However, one English company, the East India Company, did not have to pay this new tax. This meant they could afford to sell their tea cheaply in America, undercutting the American tea merchants but still making a profit.

In protest, a group of unhappy colonists (dressed as Indigenous Americans) boarded three ships in Boston in December 1773 and dumped 342 crates full of tea belonging to the East India Company (worth £11,000) into the harbour.

The British responded to what became known later as the 'Boston Tea Party' by closing Boston harbour, causing even more anger. When the British also banned all town meetings, the colonists met in secret. In September 1774, 56 representatives from the colonies met in Philadelphia to decide what to do. This meeting is known as the 'First Continental Congress' the US parliament is still known as Congress today).

Delegates at the Congress didn't decide to fight the British, but spoke out against taxation and criticised the presence of British soldiers in the colonies. They agreed to meet again in May 1775, but in April a clash between colonists and British troops led to the outbreak of all-out war: the War of Independence.

Meanwhile... 1774

In October 1774, 51 women in Edenton, North Carolina, signed and published a statement declaring that they would stop buying all British goods. This was important as, in many households, women took decisions about which household goods to purchase. It was the first time that a large group of women had collectively taken political action in US history. It is known as the Edenton Tea Party.

War

The British sent soldiers to force the rebels to stay loyal to Britain. They were met with fierce resistance. In June 1775, George Washington was appointed as the leader of the Continental Army. A year later, in July 1776, Congress met again and formally declared themselves independent from Britain.

The American War of Independence

The fighting took place from 1775 to 1783. It was bloody and brutal, and both sides lost thousands of soldiers. After one heavy defeat in Yorktown, the British Prime Minister at the time (Lord North) broke down and cried. Eventually, however, the Americans won. The 13 colonies joined together to form the United States of America. A few years later, in 1789, this new independent country appointed its first President, George Washington.

The Declaration of Independence

Signed on 4 July 1776 (now known as Independence Day), this document was drawn up by white American men and stated that 'all men are created equal'. However, the declaration does not condemn or abolish slavery – in fact, the only mention of enslaved people is when it accuses the British of stirring up slave rebellions. In addition, the declaration shows the racist attitudes of the colonists as it refers to Indigenous Americans as 'merciless Indian savages'. The declaration also does not mention women, who were still not allowed to vote.

▶ **SOURCE A** The first flag of the USA was made up of 13 stars and stripes to symbolise the 13 colonies.

Fact ✓

African-Americans were involved on both sides of the war – up to about 8,000 on the side of the colonists, and about 20,000 for Britain. The British promised freedom to enslaved Africans who fought for them. Many Indigenous peoples tried to stay neutral, but some joined the war effort.

Key Words: taxed

▼ **SOURCE B** The Declaration of Independence, signed 4 July 1776.

Over to You

1. Imagine you are an American colonist in 1773. Write to your cousin in Britain explaining why colonists are unhappy with the British government, and what the Boston Tea Party was all about.

2. a) Create a timeline (1773 to 1789) of events relating to the American War of Independence.
   b) Many US citizens today call the Declaration of Independence one of their 'founding documents'. What do you think this means?

Significance

1. Describe:
   - The Boston Tea Party
   - The Edenton Tea Party
2. Explain the significance of these two events.

1 Have you been learning?

🔄 Quick Knowledge Quiz

Choose the correct answer from the three options:

1. What was the estimated Indigenous population of North America in the late 1400s?
   a one million to three million
   b three million to seven million
   c seven million to ten million

2. In what year did Christopher Columbus first sail to the Americas?
   a 1492   b 1592   c 1692

3. Which British explorer organised voyages to North America in 1584, 1585 and 1587 in the name of Queen Elizabeth I?
   a Walter Raleigh
   b John Cabot
   c Humphrey Gilbert

4. What was the name of the British colony founded in Virginia, North America, in 1607?
   a Kingston
   b Jamestown
   c Maryland

5. Which war, lasting from 1756 to 1763, was fought mainly between Britain and France for control of North America?
   a War of Independence
   b Boston Tea Party
   c Seven Years War

6. In what year did British traders first become involved in the trade in enslaved Africans?
   a 1492   b 1562   c 1607

7. By the 1760s, how many British colonies were there in North America along the eastern coast, stretching back from the Atlantic Ocean to the Mississippi River?
   a 13   b 15   c 17

8. The protest against cheap tea imports that took place in December 1773 is commonly known by what name?
   a Edenton Tea Party
   b First Continental Congress
   c Boston Tea Party

9. The Declaration of Independence was signed on what date in 1776?
   a 4 July   b 14 July   c 24 July

10. Which of the following best describes the term 'empire'?
    a the first people who lived in any region or country
    b a collection of communities, regions, territories or countries ruled over by one leader or 'mother country'
    c a group of people who live in the same area and share the same language, culture and history

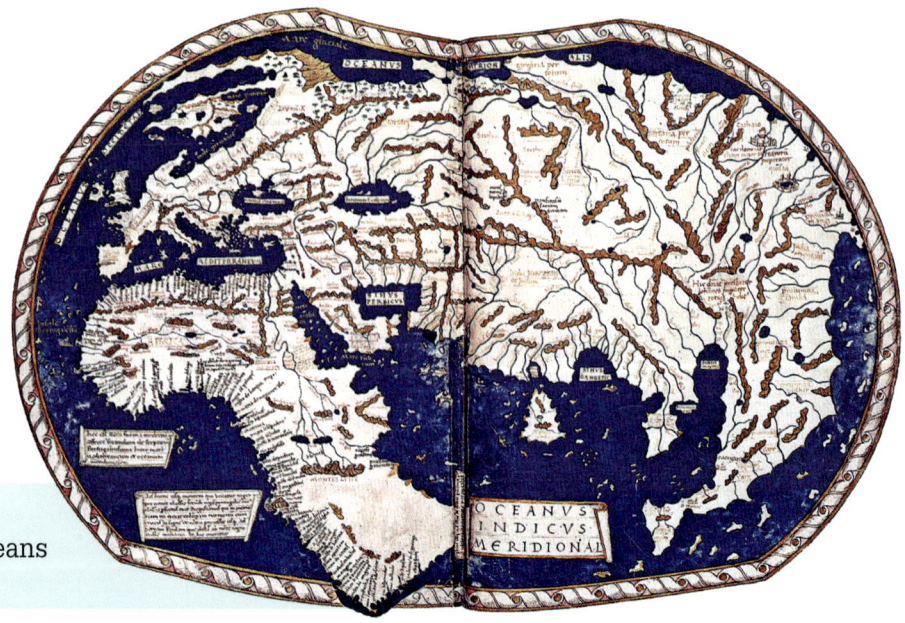

▶ **MAP A** A map, by Henricus Martellus from around 1489, showing what Europeans thought the world was like at that time.

30 | Chapter 1: British America

Have you been learning?

▶ **MAP B** A map of the world showing the seven continents.

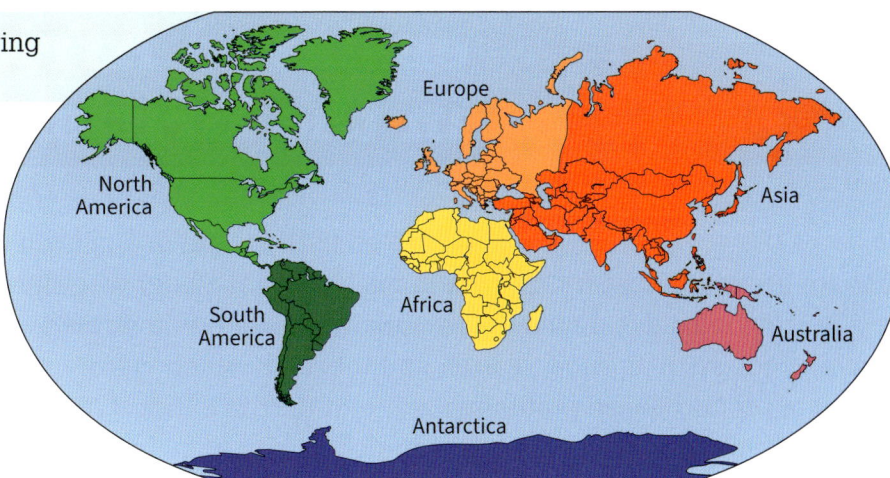

Mapping the world

1. **a** What major continents and oceans featured on the modern world map are not found on the Martellus map of 1489? You might need to use an atlas to help you.
   b Why do you think these major continents and oceans are not found on the older map?
   c Look at the outline of Africa on the older map. Why do you think there are so many place names along the northern and western coasts of Africa, but hardly any on the eastern coast?
   d Write a sentence or two about the role played by each of the following in the early years of the British Empire:
   - John Cabot
   - Queen Elizabeth I
   - Walter Raleigh
   - King James I
   - Seven Years War

Odd two out

2. Here are five paragraphs about the colonisation of North America. Each paragraph has two errors. One is a spelling mistake and the other is a factual error. When you have spotted the mistakes, write each paragraph out correctly.
   a The Indigenous peoples of North America were generally grouped into tribes or nations, based on the area or region in which they lived and their shared customs, culture, language and religion. There were hundreds of tribes throughout North America when John Cabot first arrived in 1492, speaking many different languages and dialects.
   b In 1578, King James I gave permission to Humphrey Gilbert to travel to North America and build a colony. The settlers hoped to farm, fish and perhaps find gold. Gilbert's first voyage never reached North America, but in 1583, Gilbert tried again. After landing in North America, he claimed ownership of hundreds of miles of land for the Queen.
   c The first few attempts by English settlers to set up colonys in North America were failures. However, all that changed in 1607 when a new colony called Elizabethtown became the first permanent English settlement in North America.
   d The colonies in North America were an important part of the British Empire for many years. The colonists grew tobacco, coton and many other crops that they sold back in Britain and Europe. But eventually the colonists in America decided to break free from British rule and in 1876 they declared their independence.
   e The American War of Independence lasted for several years. Thousands of troops from Britain went over to fight the rebel colonists. Finally, though, the colonists won and the 14 British colonies in America became independent.

British Empire 31

Big Question 4: Why was the trade in enslaved Africans abolished in the British Empire?

By the early 1800s, Britain had been involved in the trade in enslaved Africans for around 250 years. The trade made Britain a very wealthy country. It provided slave owners with unpaid workers who farmed expensive goods such as sugar, cotton and tobacco, which were sold for huge profits. These profits helped fund Britain's Industrial Revolution, which made the country even richer. However, in 1807, Parliament passed a law that made it illegal for any British person or ship to transport and trade in enslaved people. Yet enslaved people who were already in the colonies were not made free, and could still be bought and sold by local slave owners. In 1833, Parliament banned slave ownership too. So, why did Parliament do this? Why was the trade in enslaved people – which had made so much money for so many people – banned? And what were the most important factors that played a part in ending the trade?

Objectives

- Recall when both the trade in enslaved Africans and slave ownership ended in Britain.
- Outline the different factors that contributed to the abolition of the trade in enslaved Africans.

The beginning of the end

When Britain first became involved in the trade in enslaved Africans, it was legal to make money from it. All sorts of people were involved – factory and mill owners, ship owners, bankers, investors and merchants, even members of the Royal Family. For example, Charles II was a partner in a company that transported 60,000 enslaved Africans between 1680 and 1688.

But some people felt the slave trade was wrong – and by the late 1700s, campaign groups were being set up to try to ban it. This anti-slavery movement was very important – but was the trade banned just because of this, or were there other reasons why it ended? Your challenge is to look through the following factors very carefully and try to form your own thoughts on what might answer the question 'Why was the trade in enslaved Africans abolished?'

▶ **SOURCE A** In 2007, a special edition £2 coin was made to commemorate the 200th anniversary of the abolition of the trade in enslaved Africans. Have you ever seen one of these coins?

Factor 1: The trade in enslaved Africans wasn't making as much money as it used to

Some people have argued that the decision to get rid of the trade was made easier for Parliament because the trade was making less money than before. In the 1770s, the price of sugar dropped. Many of the large British-owned Caribbean plantations (large farms) that produced sugar couldn't make a profit and closed down. And with fewer sugar plantations, fewer enslaved people were needed. In 1771, plantation owners in Barbados bought 2,728 enslaved people from Africa. The following year they bought none.

So, with fewer people making enormous profits, there were fewer people to argue in favour of keeping the trade. Also, some people claimed that enslaved people didn't work as hard as people who got paid for their work. They said enslaved people had no reason to work as hard as possible because they didn't get any rewards or bonuses.

▼ **SOURCE B** Adapted from what the famous Scottish economist Adam Smith wrote about the trade in enslaved Africans in 1776 in his book *The Wealth of Nations*.

'The work done by slaves, though it appears to cost only their maintenance [food and shelter], is in the end the most expensive of any. A person who can gain no property can have no other interest but to eat as much and to work as little as possible. Whatever work he does can be squeezed out of him by violence only.'

Earlier on... 1807

Britain was one of the first European countries to ban the trade in enslaved Africans (Denmark was the first). After 1807, Royal Navy ships patrolled the West African coast trying to stop slave ships and free the Africans on board. Known as the West Africa Squadron, it has been estimated they freed around 150,000 captured Africans over 50 years of patrols.

Factor 2: Enslaved people helped end the trade

Other people have argued that it was the actions of enslaved people themselves that helped end the trade. In 1791, enslaved people took control of the French-controlled Caribbean island of Saint-Domingue. They were led by an inspirational and formerly enslaved man named Toussaint L'Ouverture. The islanders defeated the British and then French troops who were sent to regain control.

In 1804, the island was renamed Haiti, and the people there declared independence and outlawed slavery. A common racist view at the time was that Africans were inferior to Europeans and that their natural role was to follow orders and do simple, manual work. What had happened in Haiti had proved to many people that this argument was wrong.

Big Question

Key Words economist

▼ **SOURCE C** A portrait of Toussaint L'Ouverture on a Haitian banknote. L'Ouverture studied the military campaigns of Roman emperors, and was a forceful leader with great organisational skills.

Later on...  1825

To guarantee that the French would not invade Haiti again, and to compensate the French slave owners, in 1825 the government in Haiti agreed to pay $21 billion (in today's money) to the French government. It took Haiti 122 years (until 1947) to pay this debt.

Over to You

1. Write a sentence explaining what the word 'abolished' means.
2. What's the difference between the anti-slavery law passed in 1807 and the one passed in 1833?
3. Look at **Source B**. What point is Smith making about the trade in enslaved Africans?
4. a Who was Toussaint L'Ouverture?
   b Suggest a reason why his story is important in the history of the end of the trade in enslaved Africans.

British Empire

Why was the trade in enslaved Africans abolished in the British Empire?

Factor 3: African campaigners

Many people in Britain – from doctors and lawyers to factory and mill workers – thought that slavery was acceptable. Racist views at this time meant some white people considered Black people (and people of colour in general) as less important or intelligent than themselves, and used these beliefs to help them justify the trade in and ownership of enslaved Africans.

However, several formerly enslaved people campaigned tirelessly to convince British people that the trade was wrong. For example:

- Olaudah Equiano had been taken from his home in Africa to Barbados aged 11. He worked as a servant to a ship's captain, travelled widely, and learned to read and write while in England. He was then taken to North America and sold once more but, through incredible hard work and patience, he bought his freedom and moved back to Britain, where he wrote his life story in 1789. This was widely read and turned many people in Britain against the trade.
- Mary Prince was born into an enslaved family of African descent in Bermuda and was bought and sold several times in her early life. In 1828, Prince arrived in London with a white family and managed to escape from their house. In 1831, Prince's story was published – the first published account of enslavement from a Black woman's perspective. **Source D** appears in the final chapter of her story.

Accounts like these highlighted the horrific treatment experienced by enslaved people and convinced many that the trade should be totally banned. Also, the fact that the people who wrote these accounts were clearly intelligent and articulate destroyed the claims that Africans were inferior and only suited to manual work.

▼ **SOURCE D** From *The History of Mary Prince, related by herself*, 1831.

'All slaves want to be free – to be free is very sweet. I will say the truth to English people who may read this history... I have been a slave myself – I know what slaves feel – I can tell by myself what other slaves feel, and by what they have told me. The man that says slaves be quite happy in slavery – that they don't want to be free – that man is either ignorant or a lying person.'

▼ **SOURCE E** A copy of Olaudah Equiano's bestselling 1789 autobiography. He toured Britain raising awareness of the slave trade, and his tales of cruelty changed many people's attitudes. With another formerly enslaved person, Ottobah Cugoano, he formed a group called the Sons of Africa and met MPs to persuade them to abolish the trade.

Factor 4: The anti-slavery campaigners

Some people believe it was the actions of some Europeans that had the most impact on the ending of the trade. Granville Sharp, for example, helped formerly enslaved people in court cases against those who had bought and enslaved them, and helped bring the injustice of slavery to public attention. In 1787, a group of strict Christians formed the Society for the Abolition of the Slave Trade. This group, including Sharp and a man named Thomas Clarkson, collected evidence of the horrors of the trade and the treatment that enslaved people faced. The campaigners, who believed that the trade went against Christian teachings, used this evidence to collect signatures from the public on huge petitions.

They also convinced the politician William Wilberforce to make speeches against slavery in Parliament. Between 1789 and 1806, Wilberforce made many long speeches in Parliament calling for a law to end the trade.

Big Question

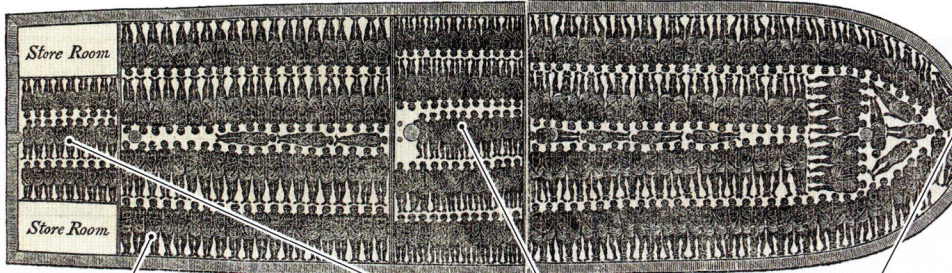

▶ **SOURCE F**
This powerful image shows how many enslaved Africans could be packed into the slave ship *Brookes*. This picture was used by anti-slavery campaigners, including Thomas Clarkson, to demonstrate the terrors of the trade. It appeared in newspapers, books and posters across Britain.

Enslaved people were shackled together in rows, lying on their backs or sides. Most had only about 30cm of space around them.

Men were loaded in the bow (front of the ship), boys in the centre, and women and young girls in the stern (back).

The diagram shows how some of the 482 enslaved people were packed into the ship. On one occasion it carried 609 people.

Food and water were kept in the hold below the enslaved people. It was rationed so it would last the whole journey.

The end of the trade in enslaved Africans

Eventually, after years of campaigning, the British Parliament abolished the trade in enslaved people in 1807. But this didn't mean owning enslaved people was banned. So, the campaign to end the trade completely continued. Famous campaigners at this time included Elizabeth Heyrick, Anne Knight, Mary Lloyd and Elizabeth Pease Nichol, who encouraged other women to set up anti-slavery groups around Britain (there were over 70 women's groups in the 1820s). A well-known tactic of the women's groups was to encourage British people not to buy or use goods produced by enslaved people, particularly sugar. In fact, around 300,000 people stopped buying sugar and the drop in sales affected the plantation owners badly. Finally, in 1833, Parliament passed the Slavery Abolition Act, granting all enslaved people in the British Empire their freedom.

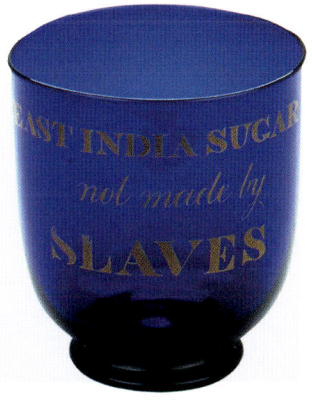

▶ **SOURCE G** A sugar bowl inscribed with 'East India Sugar not made by slaves'. Sugar bowls like this were commissioned by abolitionist societies to support and promote the sugar boycotts.

Later on...

When slave ownership ended in the British Empire in 1833, the government paid out £20 million (around £16 billion in today's money) to former slave owners for their 'loss of property'. The Bishop of Exeter, for example, received over £12,000 in 1833 for the loss of 665 enslaved people he owned with his business partners in the Caribbean. Many former owners of enslaved people went on to use their compensation money to set up or invest in businesses – and lots of these businesses still exist today.

Over to You

1. Write a sentence or two about the role played in the abolition of slavery by the following people:
   - African writers (Olaudah Equiano, Mary Prince)
   - British campaigners (William Wilberforce, Thomas Clarkson)
   - female anti-slavery groups

2. Look at **Source G**. Design your own household object that campaigns for the abolition of slavery. Remember to include an eye-catching image and slogan.

Significance

1. Make brief notes on the four reasons or factors that led to the abolition of slavery.

2. 'The main reason for the abolition of slavery was that slavery wasn't making money any more.' How far do you agree with this statement?
   HINT: You don't have to agree with the statement, as long as you can explain why you think another reason is more important.

2.1 What was India like before the British invaded?

India today is an independent country in Asia. For thousands of years, people from all over the world have settled in India, or tried to conquer it. For example, Alexander the Great (King of Macedonia, which had conquered the Greek Empire) invaded it, and the Chinese went to India in pursuit of knowledge and to visit the ancient universities. The Mughals, from Central Asia, invaded in the 1500s and then, in the 1600s, came the French, the Dutch, the Danes, the Portuguese … and also the British. This chapter looks at why India was so appealing to foreign countries, how it was colonised by Britain, and how India regained its independence in 1947.

Objectives
- Describe what India was like before the British invaded.
- Explain why India was targeted by the British.

Incredible India

Today, India shares its borders with six countries – Pakistan to the northwest; Nepal, China and Bhutan to the north; and Myanmar (Burma) and Bangladesh to the east. India is the world's largest democracy and second most populated country.

India is rich in natural resources – iron ore, silk, copper, gold, silver, gemstones, tea and timber. Spices (which were very valuable in the Middle Ages) are common in India too. This meant that any country that made strong trade links with India could potentially become very rich and powerful. Any country that managed to take control of India could become even more so.

The word 'Indian' is used to mean the people who live in the subcontinent of India – in the modern-day countries of Bangladesh, Bhutan, India, Nepal, Pakistan and Sri Lanka.

Fact ✓
Rani Mangammal was a famous queen regent (reign 1689–1705) who ruled over the Madurai Nayak Kingdom on behalf of her infant grandson. She is remembered as a wise military commander, and a great builder of roads, temples and resting places for travellers.

A cultural and religious centre

Three of the world's major religions – Hinduism, Buddhism and Sikhism – originated in India. It is also home to millions of Muslims, Christians and people of other religions. Since ancient times science, technology, art, literature, mathematics, and religion have flourished in India.

The rulers of India

Before many European nations began to sail to the East, India as we know it today did not exist. It was divided into lots of kingdoms. Most were run by Hindu princes. Occasionally the kingdoms would go to war against each other – but there were long peaceful periods too. However, in the early 1500s, the Mughals, who were Muslims, invaded many of these kingdoms and took control.

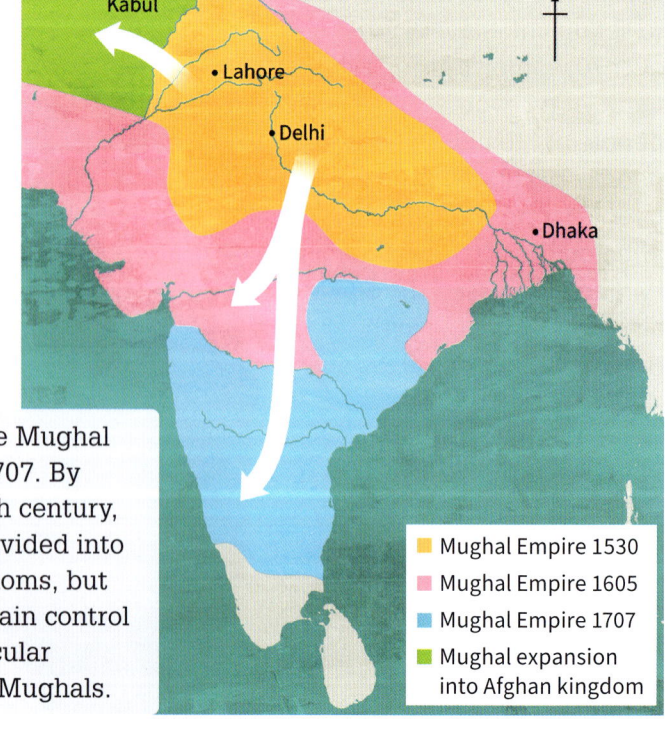

▶ **MAP A** The Mughal Empire to 1707. By the sixteenth century, India was divided into lots of kingdoms, but under the main control of one particular group – the Mughals.

- Mughal Empire 1530
- Mughal Empire 1605
- Mughal Empire 1707
- Mughal expansion into Afghan kingdom

▼ **SOURCE B** The Jama Masjid in Delhi is one of the largest mosques in India. It was built by Mughal Emperor Shah Jahan between 1650 and 1656.

▶ **SOURCE C** Gateway in the Buddhist complex at Sanchi in Madhya Pradesh, India. This was carved in the first century BCE.

▶ **SOURCE D** The Golden Temple in Amritsar, India – the holiest place of worship for Sikhs, built in the late 1500s.

▼ **SOURCE E** Sri Ranganathaswamy Hindu Temple in Tamil Nadu, India. It was built and rebuilt from the third to seventeenth centuries.

Within decades, the powerful Mughal emperor, Akbar, had managed to unite many of the Indian states and ruled over all the Hindu princes. He was well known for his religious tolerance and knowledge of literature and great architecture. This was a time when India became incredibly wealthy. For example, in 1600, Britain was producing about 2 per cent of all the world's goods and services, while India was generating around 25 per cent.

The Mughal emperors mainly ruled peacefully. They embraced local cultures and influenced art, cuisine and architecture. However, Akbar's great-grandson, Aurangzeb, was a more ruthless ruler, executing political opponents and imposing taxes on non-Muslims. As wars over control and land broke out all over India, the Mughals were losing command of the country by the early 1700s. It was at exactly this time, when much of India was at war, that European nations became very interested in controlling the country.

European interest

Several European nations saw the conflict in India as an opportunity to increase their own influence there. Many nations, but mainly the Dutch, French and British, realised that by helping certain Indian princes – with weapons and soldiers, for example – they could affect the outcomes of the wars as they wanted. Then, when the kingdom they helped was successful, they could demand rewards from the prince – perhaps land or goods. European countries could even fight against the Indian princes and take their lands for themselves.

Over to You

Plan a presentation called 'Incredible India'. Include details of India's eventful history and rich culture, and explain why European nations took an interest in it. Include text, images and/or film clips. Use no more than 250 words.

Source Analysis

Give two things you can infer about India before the British invasion from **Sources B to E**.

2.2 The invasion of India

In 1497, Portuguese explorer Vasco da Gama discovered how to sail to India from Europe by sea. Soon, many European countries were sending ships to India to trade. At first the ships simply reached an Indian port and bartered with local traders, swapping items such as guns, swords or shoes for silk, spices or tea. The European traders then brought these home with them to sell for a big profit. So, how did this early trading system develop into a British invasion?

Objectives

- Define how trade in Indian goods worked in the seventeenth and eighteenth centuries.
- Explore how Britain began to control large parts of India.

Trading stations

With the permission of local Indian rulers, the traders began to set up more permanent bases along the Indian coast. Known as **trading stations**, these large warehouses were surrounded by huge fences and guarded by men with guns. The goods were stored in the warehouses, and this was where the trading took place. Sometimes the traders lived there with their families too.

There were often workshops or 'factories' within these trading stations that turned some of the raw materials into goods. Cotton cloth, for example, was woven by Indian weavers and exported by the British in huge quantities to supply the demand for cheap, washable, lightweight fabric. Opium, an addictive drug, was also grown and sold by British traders in China at a massive profit.

Earlier on... 1600S

When the British first started trading there, people used the word 'India' to mean the present-day countries of Pakistan, Myanmar, Bangladesh Afghanistan, Sri Lanka and Nepal – as well as the present-day country of India itself.

The East India Company

In the early years of European trade with India, the main countries with trading stations were France, the Netherlands and Britain. The British trading stations were run by one company – the East India Company (EIC). Set up in 1600, it sent ships all over the world for many years. The ships left Britain full of cheap British goods, and traded them for goods such as fine china, silk, coffee and spices in countries as far away as Japan, China and, of course, India. Then they brought these goods back to Britain to sell at high prices. The business people in charge of the Company, and the kings and queens to whom they paid taxes, all made a fortune from this trade.

Later on... TODAY

The Koh-i-Noor is one of the largest cut diamonds in the world. It is part of the British Crown Jewels. The diamond may have been mined in India but there are many theories about its original owner. It was owned by various rulers in south and west Asia before being taken by the British in 1849. Since the late 1940s, India, Pakistan, Iran and Afghanistan have all demanded its return from the UK.

Later on... 2018

In 2018, an Indian economist named Utsa Patnaik calculated that Britain took a total of nearly $45 trillion from India between 1765 and 1938. Here's how it worked: the EIC collected taxes in India, then used some of this money to buy Indian goods (textiles, spices, etc.) that were then sold by the British all over the world. In short, the British bought Indian goods using money they had just taken in taxes from the Indians themselves.

38 Chapter 2: British India

Fighting begins

The East India Company first set up trading posts in India in Surat (1612), Madras (1638) and Bombay (1668). In the 1700s, the EIC began to take great areas of Indian land on which they built forts to protect their trading posts. Money raised from the land funded their private army and navy, which were used against various regional rulers of India. For example, at the Battle of Plassey in 1757, around 3,000 EIC troops (2,200 of whom were local Indians) led by Major-General Robert Clive defeated an Indian army of over 40,000, led by local prince Siraj-ud-Daula. The Indian prince was supported by a number of French troops because, at this time, Britain was at war with France in the Seven Years War (see page 21).

This victory, and another one in 1764 (the Battle of Buxar), allowed Britain to expand further into India, and take over areas such as Bengal and Bihar, some of the richest parts of India. Britain continued to fight against France (and the Netherlands) and take over their trading posts and settlements in Asia too.

Robert Clive

Robert Clive was a decorated soldier and commander. He was also one of the most ruthless and personally plundered all he could from India. After the Battle of Plassey, Clive took £2.5 million in precious jewels, gold and silver from the defeated Indians. He took some for himself and transferred even more to the EIC (in today's currency, around £23 million for himself and £250 million for the Company). As Governor of Bengal, his greed and mismanagement increased the devastation of the 1770 Bengal famine, in which around ten million people died. He was a controversial figure in Britain at the time, earning the nickname 'Lord Vulture'. There were also attempts in Parliament to strip him of his title and wealth.

The invasion continues

Over the following decades, various Indian rulers were either beaten in battle or played off against each other, so that more of India came under British rule. In the late 1700s, American colonists successfully fought for their independence from the British Empire (see pages 28–29). After this, India was seen as a vital part of the British Empire and a replacement for the 'lost' American colonies. By the late 1700s, most of India was controlled by the British – the EIC became notorious for its corruption, violence and high taxes, and many Britons who worked for the EIC lived in great luxury in India and made immense fortunes.

Key Words trading station

▶ **SOURCE A** This statue of Robert Clive was erected in 1916 in London. Although it caused controversy when it was built because of Clive's behaviour in India, it still stands today.

▼ **INTERPRETATION B** A 2020 tweet by Shashi Tharoor, an Indian politician and writer.

'a statue of Robert Clive still stands a mere 100m from Downing St. A memorial to a ruthless, dishonest, unprincipled leader of an unregulated corrupt corporation that oversaw India's plunder & loot (a word they stole from us, along with much of our wealth)...'.

Over to You

1. **a** What was a trading station?
   b List the European countries that set up trading stations in India in the 1600s.
   c Why were these countries so interested in India?
2. **a** What was the East India Company?
   b Explain how the company gradually took control of most of India.

Cause and Consequence

1. Describe the role played by Robert Clive in the conquest of India.
2. Explain why there have been calls for the removal of his statue.

2.3 The end of Company rule

The East India Company (EIC) took control of vast areas of India in the 1700s, and made huge sums of money by taking goods and taxes. However, from the 1770s onwards, the EIC gradually began to lose its influence over India. In 1857, a major rebellion led to the downfall of the Company altogether. So, what happened to the East India Company? How did Indians resist 'Company rule'? Why were the events of 1857–1858 so important in India's history?

Objectives

- Explore the decline in power and influence of the East India Company.
- Examine resistance to British rule before 1857.

The Bengal Famine, 1770

In the late 1760s, a terrible famine hit Bengal in the eastern part of India. By early 1770, there was starvation, and deaths were occurring on a large scale by 1771. It is estimated that around 10 million people died. The East India Company made the situation much worse. It refused to offer aid and continued to collect taxes from the starving population by force. The famine also severely affected Indian industry, which in turn affected the EIC. There were fewer workers and goods, so there was less tax income for the EIC. Before long, the Company was not making the same amount of money each year as it used to, so the British government stepped in. In 1773, the British government limited some of the powers of the East India Company. In 1784, the India Act stated that both the British government and the EIC controlled the territory in India jointly.

▶ **SOURCE A** A large grain store (called the Golghar) in the eastern state of Bihar, India. It was built in the 1780s by the East India Company to store grain in case another famine hit. It was intended to be just the first of a series of huge grain stores – but no others were ever built. It was found to be unsuitable for storing grain (which rotted in the heat) and wasn't used. It is now a popular tourist destination.

▼ **INTERPRETATION B** William Dalrymple (a Delhi-based historian and author) talking with Anita Anand (a journalist and author), in Episode 2 'Company Rule in India' on a podcast series called 'Empire' (2022).

'The Company does not see itself as responsible for the people of Bengal; it is there merely to make profit. And they are very cold-hearted and clear-headed about this. They just want to gather taxes. So… even as these bodies are piling up, as flies are circling, as dogs and vultures are picking at human bodies in the street in every town in Bengal… the soldiers are being sent out into the villages to gather tax forcibly. So they're taking money from starving families as if it was a normal year. This isn't the Indian practice. The Indian practice is that you waive [stop] taxes in years of famine.'

A changing atmosphere

The British government became increasingly involved in India and gradually took more control of the EIC's affairs. There was a time when the EIC had total control over all the trade in India, but from 1813 the government allowed other companies to trade too. Before long, the EIC stopped trading altogether and simply helped the government run India and collect taxes.

At this time, groups of British Christian **missionaries** went to India to preach about Christianity. They felt that Indian traditions, customs and religions should be replaced, and tried to convert as many Indians as possible to Christianity. This led to a build-up in tension between Indians and British people.

▼ **INTERPRETATION C** William Dalrymple talking on a podcast series called 'Empire' (2022).

'Once the Brits have got supreme power, they begin to show their racism, they begin to look down on Indians, they begin to behave as if all Indians are inferior.'

Fact ✓

Some East India Company employees fully embraced Indian life and culture. Many married Indian women. In the 1780s, one in every three EIC employees left their property and money to an Indian woman. However, by 1820 this was only one in five – and by 1840 it rarely happened.

Connections

The British government tried to protect the East India Company (many British politicians had links to it). So, the government allowed the EIC to sell cheap tea in America without paying taxes. This annoyed American tea merchants who lost money because of all the cheap tea flooding into America. They protested against this – and one such protest was the Boston Tea Party of 1773 (see pages 28–29). Indeed, the tea that was thrown into Boston harbour was East India Company tea!

Cause and Consequence

Explain how the arrival of British Christian missionaries led to a build-up of tension between Indians and British people.

Key Words
missionary

Rebellion against British rule

There were often rebellions against British control of India (around 40 major ones between 1757 and 1856). However these rebellions were often sparked by local issues, such as taxation or land shortages, and generally took place only in one area or town. For this reason they didn't spread throughout India. The Sannyasi Rebellion (1770–1777), the Bhil Revolt (1818) and the Kol Uprising (1831–1832) are all examples of how Indians expressed their resentment against the British.

When, for example, the British made tax and land changes in the region of Odisha in eastern India, the farming community there rose in rebellion. They were joined by the Paikas, a peasant army that had fought for local rulers for many years. The rebels took control of the town of Khordha and forced the East India Company to retreat. However, the EIC eventually regained control and dealt brutally with the rebels. The rebellion came to be known as Paika Bidroh (Paika Rebellion) of 1817.

▶ **SOURCE D**
A statue commemorating the Paika Rebellion outside the state museum in Bhubaneswar, Odisha.

Over to You

1. How did the East India Company react to the Bengal Famine of 1770?
2. a What was the Golghar?
   b Was the Golghar effective? Explain why.
3. Suggest a reason why rebellions against British rule didn't spread across India at this time.

2.4 The First War of Independence

The East India Company employed its own British soldiers. By the 1850s, there were around 40,000 British soldiers in India. However, the EIC also employed local Indians as soldiers (called **Sepoys**). There were around 200,000 Sepoys (mainly Hindus and Muslims). However, on 10 May 1857, a group of Sepoys working for the British in Meerut, northern India, shot dead a number of British soldiers. Soon there was fierce fighting between the British and Sepoys across northern India. What were the causes and consequences of these events?

> ## Objectives
> - Outline the reasons why the First War of Independence began.
> - Examine the events and consequences of the First War of Independence.

Sepoys and rebellion

According to Queen Victoria (reign: 1837–1901), the aim of the British Empire was to 'protect the poor natives and advance civilisation'. It was clear, then, that for some British people there was more to the empire than just the financial benefits. The British felt they were 'superior' to the Indigenous peoples who were already living there. In India, the British claimed that they were improving the country, by building railways, roads, schools and hospitals, rather than exploiting it.

However, in the army, the Sepoys were very unhappy. They felt that they weren't treated well, had little hope of promotion and were often the first to be sent to the most dangerous places. Some Sepoys also felt pressured into converting to Christianity.

The spark

The conflict of 1857–1858 started as a result of what the Sepoys saw as a lack of cultural understanding by the British. In January 1857, each Indian soldier was given a new rifle that used bullets and gunpowder kept in a container called a cartridge. The cartridge was covered in grease to make it easier to slide the bullets down the gun barrel. Loading the gun quickly involved biting the top off the cartridge with your teeth. However, it was rumoured that the grease was made from animal fat, probably (but not definitely) a mixture of pork and beef fat – the worst possible mixture for Hindus and Muslims. Hindus don't eat beef because cows are viewed as sacred, and Muslims are forbidden from eating pork. Many believed that the British had done this deliberately as part of a plan to force the Sepoys to convert to Christianity.

The conflict begins

The Sepoys' objections to the new cartridges were largely ignored. And when 85 Sepoys refused to use the cartridges, they were jailed for ten years. Days later, other Sepoys rioted in support of them. Many local Indian leaders, unhappy with British interference in India, joined the Sepoys – and soon the whole of northern India was engulfed in conflict.

There were major battles between British troops and Sepoys in Delhi, Cawnpore and Lucknow and both sides acted brutally. The conflict lasted around 18 months and it ended in July 1858 when the British, helped by Indian soldiers who remained loyal, defeated the Sepoys. Revenge was violent, bloody and swift.

▼ **INTERPRETATION A** A Russian illustration from the 1880s showing the brutal punishment of rebel Sepoys, who have been strapped to a cannon about to be fired. Many other Sepoys were hanged.

▼ **SOURCE B** Lakshmibai, the Rani (Queen) of Jhansi, an area of northern India. She lost much of her land to the British and fought against them in 1857. Here she is pictured leading her troops. One of her British opponents said of her that she was 'remarkable for her bravery, cleverness and determination' and had been 'the most dangerous of all the rebel leaders'. The Indian National Army named its first female unit after her in 1942.

Key Words

Sepoy   viceroy   mutiny

▼ **INTERPRETATION C**
In an account from 1884, Vishnubhat Godse describes his experience of the British attack on the fort of Jhansi in April 1858.

'The English began entering the city and shooting down every man that they saw and setting fire to houses... They sought out males from the age of five to the age of eighty and killed them... Thousands of white soldiers entered the city from all sides and commenced massacring people. The terror in the city at this time was immeasurable.'

The end... and after

After the conflict, many people were shocked by the strength of feeling against the British in India. The British government took over full responsibility for running India from the East India Company. A new department, the India Office, was set up in 1858, and a **viceroy** was put in charge of India on behalf of Queen Victoria.

Before the rebellion, British policy introduced British ideas about religion and education – which threatened the Hindu, Muslim and Sikh ways of life. After 1858, the British tried to interfere less with religious matters, and started to allow Indians more say in the running of India by allowing them jobs in local government. However, by 1900, nine out of ten government jobs were still done by Britons – and there were still lots of restrictions on other types of jobs. Sikhs, for example, were not allowed to drive trains on the railways.

What's in a name?

Historians often give names to different events (the Peasants' Revolt, the English Civil War and so on) – but there is no universally agreed name for the events of 1857–1858. At the time in Britain, it was known as the 'Indian **Mutiny**' or the 'Sepoy Rebellion'. It is often still called this in Britain today. However, for Indians today, it is most often referred to as the 'First War of Independence' or the 'Great Rebellion'. It is looked upon as the first episode in the struggle against the British for an independent India. Indeed, in 2007 the Indian government celebrated the 150th anniversary of it with special events and ceremonies. On the Indian government website, the rebellion is covered in a section entitled the 'Indian Freedom Struggle'.

Over to You

1. What was a Sepoy?
2. List the causes of the events of 1857–1858. Try to divide them into 'short-term' and 'long-term'.
3. Look at **Interpretation A**. Why do you think the punishments were so brutal?
4. a Why do you think British politicians at the time called the events of 1857 the 'Indian Mutiny'?
   b Why do you think Indians today call the same event the 'First War of Independence'?

2.5 What was the impact of the empire on Britain and India?

India was one of the largest and richest of all the countries in Britain's empire. In 1858, a viceroy, appointed by the British, was put directly in charge of the country and ran it on behalf of Queen Victoria. The Queen even gave herself an extra title and started calling herself 'Empress of India'. India was also the colony that many British people treasured the most – even calling it 'the jewel in the crown'. So, what impact did the British make on India? What was the impact on Britain? How is the impact interpreted differently?

Objectives

- Examine the impact of the British Empire in India in the nineteenth and early twentieth centuries.
- Identify a variety of viewpoints on the British takeover of India.

Divided opinions

In the past, many people justified the British Empire in India by listing all the 'benefits' that the colonialists brought. During the time of the Raj (raj means 'rule' in Hindi), British colonialists tried to portray their takeover of India in positive terms: bringing wealth, civilisation and Christianity. Some truly believed this is what they were doing. However, this ignores both the views of colonised Indians themselves and some of the other motivations behind the 'development' of India.

Impact on Britain

It is clear that the British intended to make a lot of money from India. Perhaps the biggest impact on Britain was the boost it gave to British industry and wealth. A steady supply of raw materials from India came into Britain, which were converted into finished products in British factories and then sold back to countries in the empire, including India itself. This created jobs for British business people and merchants, sailors, dockworkers, factory workers, shopkeepers and so on, and helped fuel the industrial revolution.

British rule in India brought other benefits to Britain, most notably the Indian army. This army was used in all parts of the empire, and fought bravely and decisively in both the First and Second World Wars. It is notable that in the First World War, by December 1914 one in every three soldiers fighting for Britain in France was from India.

There were also some more subtle impacts in Britain. Tea became a popular drink and food inspired by India such as chutneys, kedgeree and mulligatawny soup became popular in Britain. Queen Victoria employed an Indian secretary, Mohammed Abdul Karim, to teach her the Indian languages Hindi and Urdu, and had Indian dishes on most dinner menus. Indian words, such as 'bangle', 'shampoo', 'pyjamas', 'cash' and 'loot', became commonly used, and many grand buildings (such as the Royal Pavilion in Brighton) were built in an Indian style.

Impact on India

There is little doubt that the British made a huge impact on India. But did this benefit Indians as the colonialists claimed? By 1900, the British had built nearly 80,000km of road, as well as railways, and dug nearly 12,000km of canal. However, these were built to make it easier to move goods for trade, and to mobilise troops, not for the benefit of the Indian people.

Fact ✓

The term 'British Raj' was used to describe the period of British rule in India between 1858 and 1947.

▼ **SOURCE A** The British Raj had its own flag.

The British colonialists built schools, universities and hospitals. However, only the privileged few benefited. Illiteracy and poverty remained widespread. Healthcare for most people was poor and famines widespread – an estimated 25 million people died in India under British rule through neglect and exploitation.

Furthermore, India suffered greatly in many other ways. British customs were forced onto people, and local traditions, cultures and religions tended to be ignored. Indian workers were often exploited, and the country's raw materials were taken back to Britain, which helped Britain to become an industrial nation. Before the British took over, India produced 25 per cent of the world's cloth. After colonisation, Britain became the centre of the cloth industry. If there was ever any resistance, the British army usually came down very hard on the rebels.

It is also important to note that we have no way of knowing how India would have developed if the British hadn't invaded. The British built the railways in India, but it is quite possible that an independent India would have built similar transport networks.

▶ **SOURCE B**
An illustration from a French newspaper about the Indian famine of the late 1800s; approximately six million Indians died – and many blamed the British for not doing enough.

▼ **INTERPRETATION C** Adapted from *Pax Britannica*, written by modern historian Jan Morris in 1968. At the time of writing, Ceylon (now Sri Lanka) was classified as part of India and was under British rule.

'Ceylon was unified under British rule in 1815. Over the next 80 years, the British built 3,700 kilometres of road and 4,600 kilometres of railway. They raised the area of land used for farming from 160,000 hectares to 1.3 million hectares, the livestock from 230,000 to 1.5 million, the post offices from 4 to 250, the telegraph lines from 0 to 2,500 kilometres, the schools from 170 to 2,900, the hospitals from 0 to 65, the annual amount of goods shipped abroad from 68,000 tonnes to 6.3 million tonnes.'

▼ **INTERPRETATION D** Adapted from an article published in a British newspaper in 2017 called "But what about the railways…?' The myth of Britain's gifts to India', written by Shashi Tharoor, an Indian politician and writer.

'The British ran government, tax collection, and law and order. Indians were excluded from all of these… The death of an Indian at British hands was always an accident, but any crime by an Indian against a British person was always dealt with severely… The construction of the Indian Railways is pointed out as a benefit of British rule, but the railways were built for Britain's benefit. British investors made huge amounts of money when the railways were built, and they were used mainly to transport Indian resources… to ports for the British to ship home to use in their factories.'

Over to You

1 Write a sentence or two explaining the following terms:
   a viceroy
   b Empress of India
   c the jewel in the crown
   d Raj
2 Suggest reasons why the British rule of India divides opinions, even today.

Source Analysis

1 Interpretations **C** and **D** give different impressions of the impact of British control of India. What is the main difference between the impressions?
   HINT: Think about what information has been left out as well as what has been included.
2 Suggest one reason Interpretations **C** and **D** give different impressions of the impact of British control of India.

2.6A Independence for India

British influence in India began in the 1600s, and over the next few hundred years, the British took control of large parts of India. In 1858, during the reign of Queen Victoria, the British government took direct control of India. The British ran many aspects of everyday life, such as education, the army, railways, and law and order. Queen Victoria proudly called herself 'Empress of India'. But less than 100 years later, in 1947, India regained its independence from Britain. How did this happen?

Objectives

- Recall key events in the campaign for Indian independence.
- Examine the role of two world wars in the ending of British rule in India.

▼ **SOURCE A** Members of the Indian National Congress, 1885.

The Indian National Congress

Many Indians believed that India should be free from British control. In 1885, a political group called the Indian National Congress (INC) was formed to bring this about. It held meetings and organised demonstrations to further its cause, but the British ignored its demands. Britain did not want India to be independent because it provided Britain with raw materials, cheap workers and lots of trade links.

The INC was particularly influential and popular in Bengal, in the northeastern part of India. The growing support for independence worried the British – they just didn't want to 'lose' India.

Fact ✓

The British used the 'divide and rule' strategy to create divisions in India among the different religious groups, regions, classes and ethnicities. For example, the British encouraged people to vote according to their religions. They also controlled the media and allowed only certain information to be published in newspapers to try to control what people thought. Also, certain areas were given more development than others. More roads and railways were developed in one region than another, for example – and this caused unrest and conflict between the regions. The British hoped that any ill feeling would be directed to different regions and religions, rather than towards the British themselves.

As a result, Lord Curzon (the Viceroy of India) announced plans to **partition** Bengal. He felt that if Bengal was split up into separate regions, it would become difficult for people to join together and form a united independence movement. This tactic is known as 'divide and rule'.

The Swadeshi movement

People in India were strongly against the partition. Many Hindus were angry that a Muslim majority province had been created. In response, Indians established the Swadeshi movement to try to reduce the profits of British companies by **boycotting** their products. For example, they refused to buy imported cloth from Lancashire or salt from Cheshire, and encouraged Indians to make cloth in their own homes instead of buying British-made material. British-run schools and courts were also boycotted. The National Council of Education was founded in Bengal in 1906 to promote science and technology – and prove that Indians could educate themselves.

▼ **SOURCE B** From a leaflet written in 1907 by Indians in Bengal, who wanted the British out.

'Can these thieves really be our rulers? These thieves ... import a huge number of goods made in their own country and sell them in our markets, stealing our wealth and taking life from our people. Can those who steal the harvest of our fields and doom us to hunger, fever and plague really be our rulers? Can foreigners really be our rulers?'

The British response

The British responded harshly to people involved in the Swadeshi movement. Any protesters faced arrest, and students who took part in boycotts were often made to leave their colleges. Once the leaders of the Swadeshi movement were arrested, it was difficult to replace them. However, in 1911, the British reversed the partition and Bengal was reunified. Also, many leaders of the future (such as Mohandas Gandhi) were inspired by the Swadeshi movement.

India and the First World War

In 1914–1918, many Indians fought alongside British soldiers in the First World War, and India gave Britain a huge amount of money, food and materials to help with the war effort. There were 1.3 million Indian soldiers who fought in the war, and over 74,000 died. In 1919, after India's significant contribution in wartime, the British made slight changes to the way India was governed. Law-making councils were set up all across India and over five million property-owning, educated Indians were given the vote. However, the British government still controlled taxation, the police, the law courts, the armed forces, education, and much more. While some Indians welcomed the changes, others were bitterly disappointed and there were many large demonstrations.

▶ **SOURCE C**
Darwan Singh Negi, one of the first Indian winners of the Victoria Cross, Britain's top bravery medal. During the First World War he fought in France in an Indian battalion of the British army.

Key Words partition   boycotting

The Jallianwala Bagh massacre

One such demonstration took place in an enclosed park called Jallianwala Bagh in the city of Amritsar (close to the Golden Temple complex – see page 37). The park was packed with around 10,000 men, women and children. However, while some people were protesting against British rule, many others had simply gathered to celebrate a Sikh festival.

The British had banned large gatherings of people, but not everyone was aware of this. Without warning, a British general ordered soldiers to block the only exit from the park and shoot into the unarmed crowd. Over 350 people were killed, and thousands more injured.

Over to You

1. Write a sentence or two to define:
   a. the INC
   b. the Swadeshi movement
   c. the 'divide and rule' strategy
2. Make a list of the ways that India contributed to British efforts in the First World War.
3. a. Read **Source B**. Who do you think the 'thieves' were?
   b. What point does the source make about British rule?

Change and Continuity

1. Describe the changes that were made to the way India was governed after the First World War.
2. Explain why some Indians might have been happy with these changes, while others might have been disappointed.

British Empire

2.6B Independence for India

Mohandas Gandhi

In the 1920s, the Indian independence movement gained more support under the leadership of Mohandas Gandhi, a Hindu and former lawyer. He believed independence could be achieved through non-violent protest. Today, this is often called 'passive resistance'. Gandhi called it 'satyagraha', which roughly translates as 'holding firmly to truth' or 'truth force'. His approach influenced future leaders like Martin Luther King and Nelson Mandela. Perhaps the most famous non-violent protest at this time was the 1930 Salt March.

The Salt March

At this time, Indians were not allowed to make their own salt – they had to buy it – and it was heavily taxed by the British government. Gandhi and 78 leaders of the independence movement marched with thousands of protesters to the coast where they began making salt from seawater. All over India, thousands of people copied Gandhi's example and began making salt – and around 60,000 people were arrested, including Gandhi.

After Gandhi was released from prison, the British accepted they had to take the calls for independence more seriously – and they invited Gandhi to London as a representative of the Indian National Congress.

▼ **SOURCE D** Gandhi, on the Salt March with Sarojini Naidu, a key figure in the independence movement. In 1925, Naidu became the first female president of the INC, and travelled to the USA to promote non-violent protest. When Gandhi was arrested during the salt tax protest, Naidu became the new leader of the campaign.

Fact
Gandhi's followers called him 'Mahatma', which in Sanskrit means 'great soul'.

Fact
The Indian National Congress first met in December 1885. In the early twentieth century, members began to support the Swadeshi movement, and by 1917, the INC had become very popular. In the 1920s and 1930s, led by Mohandas (Mahatma) Gandhi, the INC began advocating non-violent protest, including the famous Salt March of 1930.

The Muslim League was founded in 1906 to protect the rights of Indian Muslims, many of whom were worried that Hindus dominated politics. For several decades after its formation the League (led most notably by Mohammed Ali Jinnah) called for Hindu–Muslim unity in an independent, united India. However, in 1940, the League called for the formation of a Muslim state that would be separate from the independent country of India. It wanted a separate nation for India's Muslims because it feared that an independent India would be dominated by Hindus.

Towards independence

In 1935, the Government of India Act gave some self-government to India. For example, elections were introduced (where some women could vote) but India still remained part of the British Empire and was still ruled by a viceroy, appointed by the British. Many Indians, including Gandhi and the INC, continued to demand complete independence. Many Muslims in India had formed their own independence group (the Muslim League). Their leader, Mohammed Ali Jinnah, called for a new, separate country for Indian Muslims.

India during the Second World War

In 1939, Britain declared war on Germany. It also declared war on behalf of India, without consulting Indian leaders. However, as in the First World War, thousands of Indians joined up to fight as part of the British Empire forces. In total, 2.5 million Indians fought in what was the largest volunteer army in history.

The Muslim League supported the war. Many in the INC were prepared to support the war only in exchange for full independence. Others did not agree with fighting because of their non-violent beliefs.

By 1942, there was widespread discontent in India. The British were worried as Japanese forces were very close to the Indian border. In response, the British government sent Sir Stafford Cripps to negotiate with Indian leaders.

▼ **SOURCE E** Indian soldiers fighting as part of the British army with a captured Nazi flag in the Libyan desert, 1943.

▼ **SOURCE F** Subash Chandra Bose, founder of the Indian National Army, meeting Adolf Hitler in Germany, May 1942.

He asked for full cooperation in the war effort in exchange for a greater degree of self-government after the war. However, the INC wanted full independence and so no agreement was reached.

The Quit India movement

At a meeting of the Indian National Congress in August 1942, Gandhi made a call for the British to 'Quit India' immediately. He called for all Indians to peacefully resist British rule. The British responded by immediately arresting Gandhi and almost all the leaders of the INC. The British also banned public meetings.

However, the arrest of the INC leaders led to mass demonstrations, strikes and disruption around the country. Over 100,000 people were imprisoned by the British as a result. Although the Quit India movement did not lead to independence immediately, it again highlighted the strength of feeling among a huge number of Indians against the British position there.

Subash Chandra Bose and the Indian National Army

In 1941, Subash Chandra Bose, a former president of the INC, escaped India and fled to Germany. He believed that by helping Germany and Japan defeat Britain, India could gain independence. He founded the Indian National Army (INA) of around 45,000 people, mostly from Indians living abroad and Indian prisoners of war. In 1944, the INA and Japan invaded India but they suffered a heavy defeat. Despite this, Bose was very influential within India. Japanese radio stations broadcast speeches by Bose in a number of Indian languages, focusing on the difficulties facing India, such as lack of self-government and famine.

Independence for India

The calls for Indian independence continued, and by the end of the war many other British colonies (as well as India) were demanding the right to rule themselves. Britain no longer had the military strength or the wealth to hold on to them. Also, many British people felt that rebuilding Britain after the war was far more of a priority than holding on to distant colonies. By 1946, the British government had agreed that India would become independent.

Over to You

1. a Write a sentence for each of the following:
   - satyagraha
   - the Salt March
   - Mohandas Gandhi
   - Sarojini Naidu
   - the Quit India movement
   b Write a paragraph to link them together.

2. a What was the INA?
   b Many in the British government viewed the setting up of the Indian National Army as a huge blow to Britain. Why do you think they felt this?

Causation

Explain what role the world wars played in ending British rule in India.

British Empire 49

2.7 The Partition of India

In 1946, after nearly 350 years in India, the British left. India was to become independent. But what would independence look like? How was it to be achieved? And what was the legacy of what became known as the 'Partition of India'?

Objectives

- Examine the Partition of India in 1947.
- Explore the legacy of Partition.

The end of British rule in India

In 1946, Britain agreed to independence for India. However, the Indian National Congress (which was not tied to any particular religion) and the Muslim League became involved in a bitter struggle for power. The INC wanted India to be kept as one independent nation, while the Muslim League wanted India to be split into two nations: India for the Hindu population and Pakistan for the Muslim population.

Partition

The British set a date for independence – June 1948. However, in June 1947, the new viceroy, Lord Mountbatten, brought forward the date of independence to August 1947, leaving just two months to make plans. Mountbatten put pressure on the leaders of the INC and the Muslim League and Partition was agreed, though the INC was reluctant. British India would become two independent states: India (which would be majority Hindu) and Pakistan (which would be majority Muslim). Mountbatten gave the task of drawing up the boundaries to Cyril Radcliffe, a British judge who had never visited India. He had just over a month to complete this and the borders were announced two days after India and Pakistan became independent. The sudden departure of the British, and lack of preparedness on behalf of the newly born nations, meant there was no effective law and order enforcing systems in place when this happened. The result was catastrophic violence.

India and Pakistan

Areas where over half the people were Muslim became Pakistan. Areas where over half the people were Hindu became independent India. Pakistan formed two territories: East Pakistan and West Pakistan, which were over 1,600km apart (see **Map C**).

Although both parts were majority Muslim, they spoke different languages and had different cultures.

Muhammed Ali Jinnah, leader of the Muslim League, became the first leader of Pakistan. Jawaharlal Nehru, the leader of the Indian National Congress, became the first Indian Prime Minister.

Although India was to be a Hindu majority country, and Pakistan Muslim majority, many people – including Mountbatten – did not expect that there would be much movement of populations. After all, in many regions Hindus and Muslims had lived together peacefully for hundreds of years. However, many people were terrified of being a religious minority in a new country: they did not know what to expect. Some people did not want minority groups in their new country. In this atmosphere of fear and chaos, over seven million Muslims fled to Pakistan and around the same number of Hindus and Sikhs fled to India.

Severe violence erupted at this time between the different religious communities. Up to a million people lost their lives. However, many were also brave enough to offer protection to members of rival communities.

▼ **SOURCE A** A child on the walls of a refugee camp in Delhi during the Partition of India, 1947.

Chapter 2: British India

Kashmir

Before 1947, some Indian states (known as the Princely States) were not fully controlled by the British. These states were given the choice to join India or Pakistan, or remain independent.

Kashmir, a Princely State in the Himalayas, had a majority Muslim population and a Hindu ruler. The ruler, the Maharaja of Kashmir, initially wanted to remain independent. However, in October 1947 he chose to join India. War broke out between India and Pakistan over Kashmir, and the two countries have fought over the area several times since. Currently, India controls around half of Kashmir, while Pakistan controls about a third. China also controls a small area. Tensions between India and Pakistan over Kashmir continue to this day.

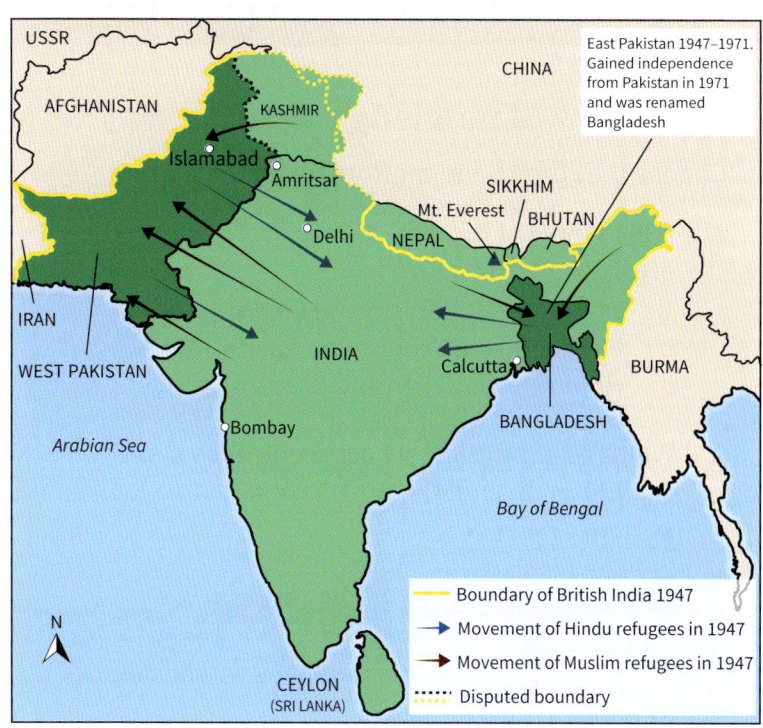

▼ MAP C How India was divided in 1947.

▼ INTERPRETATION B The trauma still lives on in the memories of those affected by the violence of Partition. From a 2022 interview with Zareena Parveen, born in 1935 into a Muslim family in the Indian city of Patiala, Punjab. Her family were among some of the 14,000 Indian Muslims killed there.

'Before Partition, our Sikh and Hindu neighbours were more like brothers and sisters… My best memories are travelling with my grandfather all over India and visiting its many hill stations… [During Partition]… My mother was slaughtered in front of my eyes, I was trapped under those bodies for three days, there was a little airway in the rubble where I could breathe… A Sikh soldier pulled me out of the rubble, and gave me food… I still pray for him… The British Raj caused this bloodshed, the British government cut us first, and then they put a Band-Aid [plaster] on… There should be an apology.'

▼ SOURCE D Pabitra Ghosh, who was displaced from modern-day Bangladesh as a child, speaking in a 2022 interview about the impact of Partition on him.

'All the Hindus in the area, we had to flee, to escape. It was a traumatic period of my life… I have been living in this country for the last 40-odd years, but that sense of rootlessness is still there… What the British did to us, dividing one country into three countries, was not a good thing, but you can't say the British alone did it.'

Over to You

1. Describe how each of the following people are linked to the Partition of India:
   a. Lord Mountbatten
   b. Cyril Radcliffe
   c. Muhammed Ali Jinnah
   d. Jawaharlal Nehru
2. Explain why India split into two countries in 1947.
3. Why did violence continue even after the split?

Later on...

Project Dastaan was founded in 2018 at the University of Oxford as a peace-building initiative. It tries to reconnect refugees of the 1947 Partition with their childhood homes in India, Pakistan and Bangladesh through first-hand accounts and virtual reality experiences.

Source Analysis

Read **Interpretation B**. Give two things you can infer about violence during Partition from this source.

British Empire

2 Have you been learning?

Quick Knowledge Quiz

Choose the correct answer from the three options:

1. Which three of the world's major religions originated in India?
   a. Hinduism, Buddhism and Sikhism
   b. Christianity, Buddhism and Sikhism
   c. Hinduism, Judaism and Sikhism

2. Which ruling Muslim dynasty controlled India from the 1500s, up until the British conquest?
   a. the Greeks
   b. the Persians
   c. the Mughals

3. When was the East India Company established?
   a. 1595
   b. 1600
   c. 1605

4. Which 1757 battle saw around 3,000 East India Company troops beat an Indian army of over 40,000, allowing Britain to expand further into India?
   a. Battle of Madras
   b. Battle of Plassey
   c. Battle of Surat

5. The East India Company employed local Indians as soldiers. What were they called?
   a. missionaries
   b. envoys
   c. Sepoys

6. In 1858, what role was created that meant that one person was in control of India on behalf of Queen Victoria?
   a. viceroy
   b. emperor
   c. rani

7. Which political group that campaigned for Indian independence was set up in 1885?
   a. Indian National Congress
   b. Liberal Party
   c. National Council of Education

8. The Salt March, the famous non-violent protest, took place in what year?
   a. 1925
   b. 1930
   c. 1935

9. What key figure in the Indian independence movement accompanied Ghandi on the Salt March (pictured below) and was the first female president of the INC?
   a. Sarojini Naidu
   b. Rani Mangammal
   c. Rani Lakshmibai of Jhansi

10. As a consequence of Partition, tensions between India and Pakistan continue to this day over which region in the Himalayas?
    a. Delhi
    b. Lucknow
    c. Kashmir

Have you been learning?

 Literacy Focus

Writing in detail

1. Look at the paragraph below. It is a very basic answer to the question 'What was the Sepoy Rebellion and why did it begin?'

   However, the answer does not contain many specific, factual details. Rewrite the paragraph to include more detail – adding names, dates, examples and facts where possible.

   > The Sepoy Rebellion was when the Sepoys rebelled. They were not happy about the way they were being treated.

   - **When did this happen? Be specific.**
   - **Perhaps mention who the Sepoys were. You could even start with this: 'The Sepoys were…'**
   - **How about dealing with the name? You might 'show off' your knowledge by mentioning that it was known as the 'Sepoy Rebellion' (or the 'Indian Mutiny') in Britain at the time, but for Indians today, it is most often referred to as the 'First War of Independence' or the 'Great Rebellion'.**
   - **Too general. It's true that the Sepoys were unhappy, but the answer does not give any more detail other than 'the way they were being treated'. This is where you go into more detail about the way they were treated. On page 42, you learned that Sepoys felt, for example, they had little hope of promotion and were being pressured into converting to Christianity. You might mention gun cartridges here too.**

Vocabulary check

2. In each group of historical words, phrases or names below, there is an odd one out. When you think you have identified it, write a sentence or two to explain why you think it doesn't fit in with the other words in its group. The first one has been done for you:

   a   Hinduism   Buddhism   (Christianity)   Sikhism

   > I have chosen Christianity because this religion did not originate in India, but the other three did.

   b   France   Brazil   Britain   the Netherlands

   c   East India Company   Sannyasi Rebellion   Bhil Revolt   Kol Uprising

   d   Delhi   Sepoy   Cawnpore   Lucknow

   e   bangle   shampoo   loot   viceroy

   f   Swadeshi movement   satyagraha   Lord Curzon   Quit India

   g   Muhammed Ali Jinnah   Cyril Radcliffe   Jawaharlal Nehru   Mohandas Gandhi

British Empire

Big Question 5: How did the British Empire change Britain at the time?

Look at **Source A**. This house was built in 1805, in Gloucestershire (in south-west England), and was paid for by Sir Charles Cockerell who made a fortune working in India for the East India Company. The house is clearly built in an Indian style, and it was filled with paintings and furniture brought back from India. It is a good example of how the empire influenced what was built in Britain – as well as the way the empire made some people so rich that they could build huge houses like this. So, during the era of empire, how else did Britain change?

Objectives
- Examine the impact of the empire on Britain.
- Assess the benefits that having an empire brought to Britain.

Making money

The empire created money-making opportunities. There were two basic ways this happened:

- Buy (or take) goods from abroad (such as sugar, tea, coffee, silk, tobacco and spices) that were hard to get in Britain, and bring them back into the country to sell for a high price. These goods were extremely popular in the days of the empire (they still are) and Britain's citizens were prepared to pay big money to smoke, drink, eat or wear them. In the mid-1800s, the tea trade alone was worth £30 million a year.

▼ **SOURCE A** Sezincote House. The house and gardens were heavily influenced by India. Note the statues of baby elephants in this picture. Shashi Tharoor, an Indian politician and writer, described the house as an 'incongruous [out of place] monument to the opulence [vast wealth] of the nabobs' loot'. 'Nabob' is a word used to describe a wealthy person who has made lots of money in India.

Trading in goods such as tea, coffee and tobacco not only made money for the traders, but created jobs in shipping, transportation and sales.

- Buy raw materials abroad very cheaply (such as cotton and rubber), then bring them back to Britain and make them into goods like clothes and tyres. Then sell these back to countries in the empire. This also created jobs for workers in Britain. In fact, by the 1830s most of the cotton worn by Indians was grown in India, made into clothing in Britain, and then sold back to Indians. As a result, British people got jobs and some British people got rich, while the Indian textile industry was destroyed.

In short, British businesspeople and traders used the empire to build up vast personal fortunes, making many of them some of the richest people in the world.

Pride

When Britain first started building its empire, ordinary British people were not particularly interested. But by the late 1800s people had become more proud of the empire. This was reflected in the popularity of songs such as 'Rule Britannia' and 'Land of Hope and Glory', as well as events such as the British Empire Exhibition (1924) which showcased the colonies to the British public. Of the 58 British colonies, 56 took part. It was the largest exhibition ever staged anywhere in the world and attracted over 25 million visitors. A purpose-built stadium was built to host it – Empire Stadium. This became Wembley Stadium.

SOURCE B An advert for biscuits from 1894.

Books and newspapers helped to fuel people's enthusiasm for the empire. Magazines for young people had such titles as *Union Jack* and *Young England*, and the popular magazine for teenagers, *Boy's Own Paper*, was filled with stories of brave soldiers 'doing their duty' while fighting on behalf of the monarch. Newspapers wrote vivid accounts of battles overseas.

The popularity of the empire at this time meant that companies were keen to associate their goods with it as a way of making more money.

Migration

For poorer British people, the empire became a way to escape unemployment and bad living conditions. Between 1800 and 1914, about 14 million people emigrated from Britain, mainly to Canada, Australia and New Zealand. People arrived in Britain from the colonies too. Many Africans, Indians and Indigenous Americans travelled to, and settled in, Britain.

INTERPRETATION C Adapted from 'Culture and Identity in Imperial Britain' by Catherine Hall (2008); as Britons included people of colour by the nineteenth century, 'Britons' in this extract refers to white Britons.

'... peoples of the empire came to Britain: African sailors, Indian servants, traders and colonial politicians all passed through and some, especially sailors and dockers, settled in Britain, establishing mixed communities in London, Cardiff, Bristol, Liverpool and Glasgow. Most Britons had seen people of colour by the mid-nineteenth century.'

Big Question

Architecture

What Britain actually looked like changed during the era of empire. Dozens of theatres, cinemas, bandstands, kiosks and piers were built in the eighteenth and nineteenth centuries that reflected a variety of 'empire styles'. Many of these buildings still exist.

Power

By the 1900s, the British Empire contained around 450 million people (approximately a quarter of the world's population) and it covered about a quarter of the world's total land area. This meant that Britain had plenty of places to keep its warships – and millions of men to call on if it went to war. Indeed, in both world wars, around 40 per cent of the men fighting for Britain were from the empire. The money generated from the empire (through taxes on trade, for example) made the country itself wealthy.

Over to You

1. Look at **Source A** and read the introduction paragraph.
   a. Who was Sir Charles Cockerell?
   b. Why do you think he built his house in this style?
   c. Explain what you think Shashi Tharoor meant when he described the house as an 'incongruous monument to the opulence of the nabobs' loot'.

2. Look at **Source B**. Why do you think British companies were so keen to associate themselves with the empire?

3. Imagine you have to explain the impact of the British Empire on Britain to a primary school student. Produce a poster, leaflet, diagram or presentation.

Cause and Consequence

Describe two ways a British person might have made money from the empire.

British Empire

3.1 What was Australia like before the British arrived?

Humans are thought to have first arrived and settled in what is now known as Australia at least 65,000 years ago (although investigations are ongoing). The original inhabitants, who have descendants living in Australia today, are known collectively as Indigenous Australians or First Nations Australians. When Europeans began to colonise Australia in the late 1700s, it was already home to perhaps 750,000 Indigenous Australians living in around 500 separate groups or 'nations'. This chapter tells the story of the British colonisation of Australia.

Objectives

- Define what is meant by the term 'Indigenous Australians'.
- Examine the culture, lifestyle and beliefs of Indigenous Australians.

Who are the Indigenous Australians?

Australia's Indigenous peoples are two distinct cultural groups but with great diversity within these groups. **Aboriginal peoples** live on mainland Australia (including Tasmania) – the world's largest island, and a continent in itself. **Torres Strait Islander peoples** live on the islands in the sea to the north east of Australia. Both groups of Indigenous Australians adapted their lives to their environment and circumstances.

Indigenous groupings

Prior to the arrival of British colonists, Aboriginal Australians used natural resources for everything they needed – food, shelter, tools, weapons and medicine. Extended family groups consisted of around 25 to 30 people, each with a specific area to hunt in. The people in these groups were very reliant on each other. Family groups were part of a nation, and at the time of the first contact with Europeans there were about 500 nations speaking around 250 different languages.

Torres Strait Islanders were farmers, who also hunted and fished for food. They are divided into five cultural groups and speak several languages.

Natural resources

Many Aboriginal peoples lived as subsistence hunters, which means they only gathered enough edible plants and killed enough wild animals and fish to meet their needs. Men hunted mainly for larger animals, such as kangaroos, emus and reptiles, while women hunted smaller animals and collected fruits, eggs and plants. Many Aboriginal nations also managed the grasslands for food and animals. They did this by a sophisticated use of fire, called 'fire stick farming', where land was burned under controlled conditions to allow it to regenerate. The majority were nomadic too, which means they moved around the countryside to hunt and gather food in tune with the seasons, rather than staying in one place. However, there is evidence that some groups established permanent settlements.

▶ **SOURCE A** An Aboriginal Australian cave painting of 'Quinkans' or spirits in Laura, Queensland. There are many rock art galleries across the region. These paintings are thought to be between 15,000 and 40,000 years old.

Caring for Country

Indigenous Australians have a deep connection to the land, water and all living things. This relationship with the natural world is linked to their belief that everything (humans, animals, rivers, hills, plants, planets, stars and so on) was created by ancient spirits – and these spirits are now part of the landscape, living on in the environment. As a result, Indigenous Australians feel a responsibility to protect the natural world. This means they only take the animals and plants they need because they want to ensure that natural resources will still be available for future generations. This view is sometimes referred to as 'Caring for Country'.

Cultural traditions

The artistic and musical traditions established by Indigenous Australians are some of the longest-surviving ones in human history. They use songs and stories, for example, to navigate the environment and locate good sources of food or water. Even the boundaries that separated one nation from another were explained via a story, rather than on a map.

▼ **INTERPRETATION B** Adapted from an interview with Aunty Beryl Timbery Beller, an Indigenous Australian of the Dharawal Nation, in 2008. Here, she refers to the arrival of British explorer Captain James Cook in 1770.

'… They were so ignorant they thought there was only one race on the earth and that was the white race. So when Captain Cook first came, he said 'oh let's put a flag up somewhere, because these people are illiterate, they've got no fences'. They didn't understand that we didn't need fences… that we stayed here for six to eight weeks, then moved somewhere else where there was plenty of tucker [food] and bush medicine and we kept moving and then come back in twelve months' time when the food was all refreshed…'

▶ **MAP C** The Indigenous Australian nations on the mainland of Australia before the British arrived. Each colour represents an area where a particular Indigenous Australian nation was based. The 'X' marks where Captain Cook landed in April 1770. The first colony was set up nearby in 1788 at Port Jackson.

Key Words

Aboriginal peoples
Torres Strait Islander peoples

Fact ✓

Indigenous Australians use natural products – wild herbs, bark and sap from trees, soil and leaves – to treat illnesses such as snake bites, jellyfish stings, headaches and burns. These treatments are known as 'bush medicine' because the ingredients were gathered from the bush (the countryside areas full of shrubs, bushes and plants).

Over to You

1. Define the term 'Indigenous Australians'.
2. Describe the relationship between Indigenous Australians and the environment.
3. What was 'bush medicine'?
4. Look at **Interpretation B**. How does this help historians understand one of the differences between British culture and Indigenous culture?

British Empire

3.2 Finding *Terra Australis Incognita*

In Australia today, you can find many places named after James Cook, including a university, schools, a river, an island and several other landmarks. His image has appeared on banknotes, stamps and coins. **Source A** below is a statue of James Cook in Melbourne, Australia. You will notice that someone has thrown paint over it. So, who was James Cook? How is he linked to the colonisation of Australia? And why has someone thrown paint over his statue?

Objectives

- Examine the early life and voyages of James Cook.
- Assess why the work of James Cook is interpreted differently.

Who was James Cook?

Born in 1728 in Yorkshire, England James Cook was a British Royal Navy commander with a reputation as an excellent ship's captain and a great map-maker.

In 1768, Cook was asked by the Royal Society (a world-famous scientific organisation) to captain a ship called *Endeavour* on a science expedition. His orders were to take a group of scientists, astronomers, botanists and artists to explore the Pacific Ocean. He was also asked to look for a great southern continent – what Europeans referred to as '*Terra Australis Incognita*' or 'unknown southern land'. European explorers knew there was land there somewhere – and had even mapped some of the west coast of Australia – but they didn't know quite how much land there was, and the rest had never been mapped by Europeans.

▶ **SOURCE A** This statue of Captain Cook in Melbourne, Australia, was vandalised on Australia Day in 2018 by 'Invasion Day' protesters.

Connections

Cook took part in several battles in what is now Canada during the Seven Years' War (see pages 20–21).

First encounters

Cook was helped by Tupaia, a brilliant navigator from the island of Tahiti with excellent knowledge of the Pacific Ocean. After several months at sea, *Endeavour* arrived in New Zealand in 1769 and sailed all around it – with Cook making maps as he went. Tragically, nine Māori (Indigenous New Zealanders) were killed by the British when they went out to meet the ship.

In April 1770, *Endeavour* landed on the east coast of Australia at a place that Cook named 'Botany Bay'. The area reminded Cook of South Wales in Britain, so he called the whole area 'New South Wales'. This part of Australia is still called New South Wales today. Cook planted a British flag on an island nearby and claimed ownership of the territory for Britain. He had been given instructions to only claim territory with the consent of the people already living there. Cook didn't get permission, and claimed the land anyway.

The Indigenous Australian view

The land that Cook first set foot on was already home to the Gweagal people of the Dharawal nation. Botany Bay already had a name: Kamay. They believed it was their duty to protect the land from anyone not invited to be there. Instead, any visitors (such as the British) must be *invited* onto the land. Also, in Dharawal culture, low lying white cloud can symbolise the spirits of the dead. As a result, the Gweagal people saw Cook's ship, which appeared on the coast through low lying cloud, as almost a ghost. They yelled '*warra warra wai*' at Cook, meaning 'you're all dead'. Cook presumed the words meant go away and shot at the two men, injuring one in the leg.

▶ **MAP C** James Cook's voyages.

▼ **SOURCE B** The Gweagal people first encountered by Cook were drawn by Sydney Parkinson, a Scottish artist on board *Endeavour*.

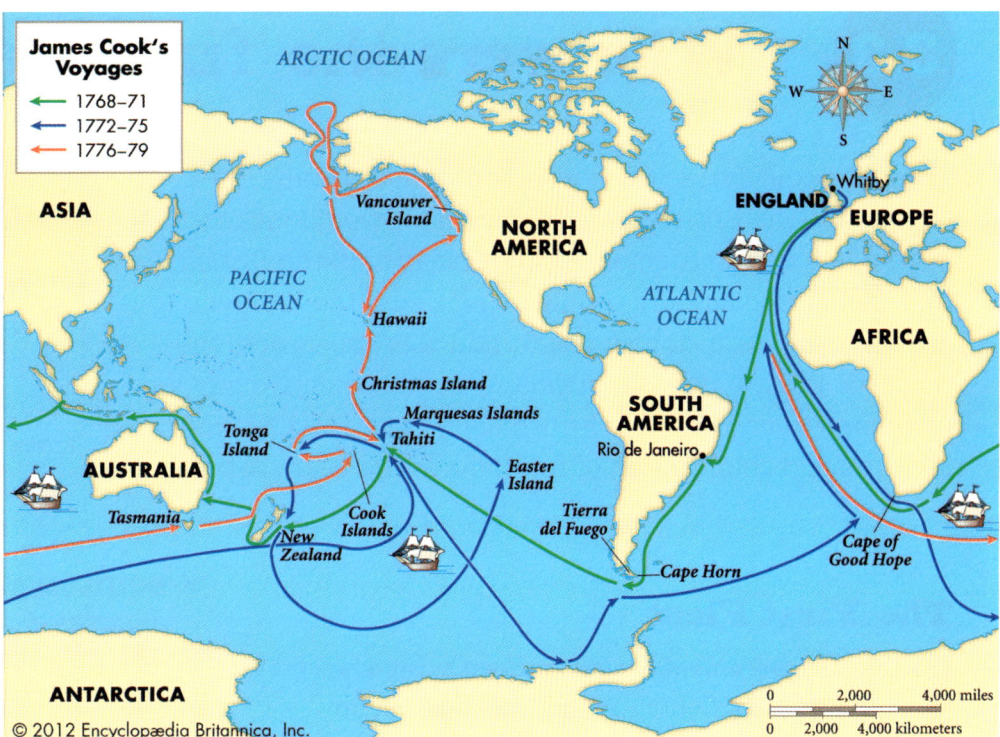

▼ **INTERPRETATION D** Written in 2022 by author Thomas Mayor, a Torres Strait Islander, in the British newspaper *The Guardian*.

Cook and his crew were largely ignored in the earliest interactions: we had no interest in trade or diplomacy with the intruders. We had everything we needed – we had and we maintained an abundance of life. Aboriginal people went about peaceful lives as we had for millennia, as the British explorer went about his business, foolishly believing he was discovering our lands, as though we were not there.

More voyages

Captain Cook made two more voyages to explore the Southern Pacific Ocean, sailing further south than any European had sailed before (see **Map C**). On Cook's final voyage he was killed by Indigenous people in Hawaii. He was buried at sea on 21 February 1779. Today, the site in Hawaii where Cook was killed is marked by a monument, and the area around it has been given to the United Kingdom, and is officially part of the UK.

Changing views of Cook

In recent years, there has been more debate about the actions and legacy of James Cook. The violence associated with his contacts with Indigenous peoples has been acknowledged. Although Cook did not set up a colony in Australia, some view his actions as the beginning of the violent colonisation of the whole continent. Some people do not think he should be honoured with places named after him and statues of him in public places.

Source Analysis

How useful is **Source B** for an enquiry into the lives of Indigenous Australians before contact with Europeans?

Over to You

1   a   What did the term '*Terra Australis Incognita*' mean?
    b   Can you suggest some reasons why it took so long for Europeans to find '*Terra Australis Incognita*'?

2   The following dates are all important in the James Cook story:

    1779; 1768; 1770; 1728; 1769

    Write each date on a separate line in your book, in chronological order. Beside each date, write what happened in that year.

3   **Interpretation D** describes the first encounters between Cook and the Indigenous Australians. Summarise the point that the author makes.

3.3 Who were the 'first fleeters'?

When Captain James Cook returned from Australia, he reported to the British government that it would make a good place for a settlement. It didn't matter to the British that there were already people living there (the Indigenous Australians) because as far as Britain was concerned, the whole country was '*terra nullius*', a Latin term meaning 'land belonging to no one'. The British used this to justify the invasion and colonisation of Australia in the years to come.

Objectives

- Define a 'first fleeter', a 'free settler' and a 'transported convict'.
- Examine why the date 26 January is interpreted differently.

The 'First Fleet'

The British government decided to send a well-known naval commander, Captain Arthur Phillip, to set up the first colony on Australian soil. They also wanted him to take more than 700 convicts from Britain's overcrowded jails to help him do it. It was hoped that these prisoners would never return to Britain – after their sentences were completed, they would be forced to stay in Australia because they wouldn't be able to get home. This type of punishment – when guilty criminals were sent to a faraway land for a number of years – was known as **transportation**.

In May 1787, 11 ships left Portsmouth heading for the British colony of Australia. There were over 1,300 people on board the ships in total, including 736 convicted criminals. These 11 ships are today known by many in Australia as the 'First Fleet'. They arrived on 26 January 1788, now known as Australia Day.

Australia Day controversy

In recent years, Australia Day has become a divisive and controversial issue. For many, including Indigenous Australians, it is known as Invasion Day and marks the beginning of the British seizure and occupation of land that had been occupied by First Nations Peoples for tens of thousands of years. A survey in 2022 revealed that a majority of Australians believed it was important to have a day celebrating the nation. 37 per cent believed that the current date (commemorating the landing of the First Fleet) was offensive. However, nearly 60 per cent supported changing the date of the celebrations to a date that is not offensive to Indigenous Australians.

▼ **SOURCE A** Invasion Day protests in Perth, Australia, on 26 January 2020. Here, protesters from all walks of life demand the end to national Australia Day celebrations.

▼ **INTERPRETATION B** Gordon Syron, an Indigenous Australian painter, speaking in 2009.

'The white race came and took our land and did not even have the courtesy to ask us or buy it. They said we weren't even human beings when they claimed our land as '*terra nullius*'. British law is alright for the British but Aboriginal law, customs, language ... have been around a lot longer than "British law".'

Transportation

The oldest convict on the First Fleet was an 82-year-old woman called Dorothy Handland. She survived the trip but is thought to have died by suicide when she saw the conditions in which she was expected to live. John Hudson, who had stolen some clothes and a gun, was the youngest convict. He was nine years old.

Chapter 3: Australia

The convicts began to build the settlement. Many convicts were assigned masters, who used them to carry out whatever work they wanted for the rest of their sentence. This was usually for seven years, fourteen years or life. Hardworking, well-behaved convicts could earn themselves an early release, while poor behaviour might end in a whipping – or an extended sentence. Over the next 30 years, British courts transported over 20,000 more convicts to Australia.

Free settlers

Life in the new settlement was tough. Few of the convicts – or their masters – knew about farming or carpentry, two of the most important skills needed in the new colony. Over time, the convicts and former convicts adjusted to the Australian landscape and set up small farms. In 1790, a few free settlers landed in Australia. From the 1820s, more free settlers began to arrive from Britain, attracted by the idea of a new life in another part of the world. They brought more supplies and new skills that helped the settlement survive and grow.

▶ **INTERPRETATION C**

Captain Arthur Phillip inspecting convicts in his new colony, 1788. Captain Phillip became Governor Phillip, the man in charge of Australia's first British colony. Today, many things are named after him in Australia, including a port, several islands and many streets, parks and schools.

Fact ✓

The average age of a convict was 27. About 20 per cent of convicts were female. 70 per cent were English and Welsh, 25 per cent Irish, 5 per cent Scottish. 80 per cent were thieves. Most had been convicted several times; about 5 per cent had committed violent crimes.

Key Words transportation

▼ **SOURCE D** The first British colony in Australia, painted around 1803. It was named Sydney after a British politician. Note the Indigenous Australians looking down on the colony.

Connections

The Tolpuddle Martyrs were six farm workers (from the village of Tolpuddle in Dorset, England), who were convicted of swearing a secret oath as members of a workers' union in 1834. This was illegal at the time. They were transported to Australia, but pardoned in 1836 after mass protests and demonstrations in England. They returned to England between 1837 and 1839.

Over to You

1 a What did the British mean when they declared Australia 'terra nullius'?

   b Suggest reasons why Indigenous Australians might find this offensive. Use **Interpretation B** to help you.

2 a What was transportation and why was it introduced?

   b Who were the 'first fleeters' and the 'free settlers'?

Knowledge and Understanding

Explain why many people disagree with Australia Day celebrations.

British Empire

3.4A The colonisation of Australia

The oldest human remains discovered in Australia were found in 1968 at Lake Mungo in New South Wales, around 750km from Sydney. This site has been occupied by Indigenous Australians for at least the last 47,000 years. When the British arrived (1788), there was an estimated Indigenous population of 750,000 people in Australia. However, the British belief that Australia was a 'land belonging to no one' ('*terra nullius*') meant they believed they had a right to invade and take possession of the land. So, how did this happen? Was there conflict between Indigenous Australians and the British? What impact did this have on the Indigenous population?

Objectives

- Examine the conflict between Indigenous Australians and the British.
- Explain the impact of British settlement on both the Australian environment and the Indigenous Australian people.

British expansion

In the first few decades after the British arrived, they began to take over different parts of Australia. They set up farms and looked for gold and valuable gemstones like opal. This caused many problems for the environment. For example, miners dug up the land and polluted streams and rivers. Farmers cleared land so they could grow food and did not take care to protect the Australian plants and animals.

New settlements were set up in Hobart (1803), on the Brisbane River (1824), on the Swan River (1829), on Port Phillip Bay (1835) and on Gulf St Vincent (1836). By this time, the British population in Australia was around 130,000. Today, the major cities of Hobart (in Tasmania, the island south of mainland Australia), Brisbane, Perth, Melbourne and Adelaide are found on or near these sites.

A new generation

Australia was first used by the British mainly as a place to send their criminals – but things started to change when convicts decided to stay at the end of their sentences. Some became farmers. An 'Australia-born' generation grew up too – people who were born in Australia and regarded themselves as 'Australian'. And with more 'free settlers' arriving, the population of Australia grew to 405,000 by 1850. By now the colonies each had their own councils and governors taking decisions on how to run things. Soon, this new generation of Australians began to object to Britain sending criminals to Australia. Transportation ended in 1868 – by which time a total of 162,000 convicts had been sent to Australia on 806 'transport ships'.

▶ **INTERPRETATION A**
A painting by Gordon Syron called *Invasion Day 2018*. Syron has created more than 150 paintings showing the invasion and colonisation of Australia.

Chapter 3: Australia

The Frontier Wars

Many Indigenous Australians resisted the arrival of the British colonists. This series of conflicts and battles is commonly known as the Frontier Wars and lasted from 1788 until the 1930s. One of the first leaders of this resistance was a warrior named Pemulwuy, a member of the Bidijigal nation, near what is now Botany Bay, New South Wales.

From 1792, Pemulwuy led raids on British settlements. To begin, the raiders took food, but sometimes attacked to get revenge on settlers who had attacked them. Despite a massive hunt for Pemulwuy and his followers, he avoided capture for many years. He was once shot seven times in battle – but this just added to the rumour that Pemulwuy could not be killed by British guns. Eventually, though, Pemulwuy was shot dead in 1802 during an ambush. His head was cut off and sent to London with a letter saying that he 'was a terrible pest to the colony, but a brave and independent character'.

In Australia today, Pemulwuy is a very famous Indigenous Australian. There is an area of Sydney named after him, and a park. Other resistance fighters who led their people against the British settlers, such as Dundali, Yagan and Jandamarra, are well known too, and their stories are taught to Australian schoolchildren.

British massacres

Between the 1790s and the 1920s, there were hundreds of massacres of Indigenous Australians. For example, in 1838, at Myall Creek in northern New South Wales, white colonists murdered 28 Indigenous men, women and children. In Queensland, in 1842 and 1847, Indigenous people were given gifts of flour laced with poison. Around 150 people died as a result. However, it is really hard to know the true number of massacres because they were often covered up by the authorities.

▼ **INTERPRETATION B** From an article on an Australian educational website.

> 'The land of Aboriginal peoples was claimed under the 'legal fiction' of *terra nullius*, enabling the dispossession of Aboriginal lands… "*Terra nullius*" translates to "nobody's land", but the truth is the British claim on the land disregarded evidence documented by early settlers and explorers that, prior to colonisation, Aboriginal people had well established systems of land and water use.'

▼ **SOURCE C** An engraving by Samuel John Neele from 1803. It is believed to be the only known image of Pemulwuy.

▼ **SOURCE D** Adapted from a text by Edward Wilson, the British-born editor of an Australian daily newspaper, *The Argus*, writing in March 1856.

> 'In less than twenty years we have nearly swept them off the face of the earth. We have shot them down like dogs. Whilst pretending to offer friendship we have poisoned their food and condemned whole tribes to an excruciating death. We have made them drunkards, and infected them with diseases… We have made them outcasts on their own land, and are rapidly consigning them to destruction.'

Over to You

1. a. By 1850, in what ways had Australia changed since the British first arrived?
   b. Why did transportation end in 1868?

2. Read **Interpretation B**. Why did the British think it was acceptable to build their settlements in Australia, even if it meant conflict with Indigenous Australians?

3. a. What were the Frontier Wars?
   b. Who was Pemulwuy and why is he famous?
   c. Why do you think Indigenous Australians resisted the British invasion so strongly?

Source Analysis

a. Look at **Source D**. Summarise what the writer is saying about the British treatment of Indigenous Australians.

b. How useful is this source to a historian studying the treatment of Indigenous Australians?

British Empire

3.4B The colonisation of Australia

Impact of the Frontier Wars

Historians have argued for years over how many Indigenous Australians were killed in the various battles, acts of resistance and open massacres. Some say approximately 20,000 Indigenous people were killed and around 2,500 British were killed. Other estimates put it as high as 60,000 Indigenous people in one area of Australia alone (Queensland).

The impact of disease

Indigenous people also died from diseases (such as smallpox and measles) that were introduced by the British. Governor Arthur Phillip reported that smallpox had killed around half of the Indigenous Australians in the Sydney region within just over a year of the arrival of the First Fleet. Indeed, as a result of disease and violent conflict, it has been estimated that the Indigenous population was reduced by at least 90 per cent in south-eastern Australia by 1850.

▼ **SOURCE E** An Indigenous man called Yagan, speaking to the advocate general of Victoria in the early nineteenth century. The term 'blackfellow' can be considered offensive.

> 'Why do you white people come in ships to our country and shoot down poor blackfellows who do not understand you – you listen to me! The wild blackfellows do not understand your laws, every living animal that roams the country, and every edible fruit that grows in the ground are common property ... For every black man you fellows shoot, I will kill a white man.'

▶ **SOURCE G** Part of the Australian Prime Minister's apology to the Indigenous Australian parents and children of the 'Stolen Generations'.

The 'Stolen Generations'

In the later part of the 1800s there was an attempt in many areas to strip Indigenous Australians of their heritage and cultural identity. For example, children were taken from their families to go and live in white Christian homes, and their grief-stricken parents were made to work for white colonists. The children were forbidden to speak their own language or take part in their traditional rituals. They had to get special permission to marry when they were older or to move from place to place, and their employment was strictly controlled. These children, perhaps as many as 100,000, who were taken from their families between the late 1800s and 1969 are known as the 'Stolen Generations'. In January 2008, the whole of the country stopped to listen as Australia's Prime Minister, Kevin Rudd, officially apologised for the treatment of these children.

▼ **SOURCE F** Testimony from an Indigenous woman who was separated from her family at 12 months old. Thirteen years later they met, just once, but the woman's mother died two years after that. From the *National Inquiry into the Forced Separation of Aboriginal and Torres Strait Islander Children from Their Families*.

> 'When I first met my mother – when I was 14 – she wasn't what they said she was. They made her sound like she was stupid, you know, they made her sound so bad. And when I saw her she was so beautiful. Mum said, 'My baby's been crying' and she walked into the room and she stood there and I walked into my mother and we hugged and this hot, hot rush just from the tip of my toes up to my head filled every part of my body. That was my first feeling of love and it only could come from my mum. I was so happy and that was the last time I got to see her.'

> 'We apologise for the laws and policies of successive governments that have inflicted profound grief, suffering and loss on these, our fellow Australians.
>
> 'We apologise especially for the removal of Aboriginal children from their families, communities and their country.
>
> 'For the pain, suffering and hurt of these Stolen Generations, their descendants and for their families left behind, we say sorry.
>
> 'To the mothers and the fathers, the brothers and the sisters, for the breaking up of families and communities, we say sorry.
>
> 'And for the indignity and degradation this inflicted on a proud people and a proud culture, we say sorry.'

Indigenous Australians today

By 1900, the population of Indigenous Australians had declined to about 90,000. Today the population stands at around 800,000, making up about 3.3 per cent of Australia's population. Sadly, there are still huge inequalities in many areas of life between Indigenous Australians and non-Indigenous Australians. Indigenous Australians have a life expectancy on average eight years lower than non-Indigenous Australians. They are less likely to stay in education and are far more likely to be unemployed than non-Indigenous Australians. Clearly, there is still a long way to go in order to put the descendants of the first Australians on an equal footing with those of the non-Indigenous population.

▼ **SOURCES H** and **I** In recent years, the Indigenous Australian population has worked hard to get their own flags recognised. In modern Australia these flags have become commonly known, official flags.

The Australian Aboriginal Flag: black represents the colour of the people, red is the colour of the land and yellow is for the Sun.

The Torres Strait Islander flag: green symbolises the land and blue represents the waters of the Torres Strait. The white five-pointed star represents  the five major island groups. The white dhari is a traditional dancer's headdress and symbolises the Torres Strait Islander people themselves.

Over to You

Design a leaflet, poster or presentation about the effect of colonisation on Indigenous Australians. Make sure you include:
- a definition of the term 'Indigenous Australian'
- information about the Indigenous Australian way of life before the colonisers arrived
- reasons why Indigenous Australians and colonisers clashed
- details of the 'Stolen Generations'
- facts about Indigenous Australians today.

▼ **SOURCE J** Indigenous Australian athlete, Cathy Freeman, draped in both the Australian and Aboriginal flags after winning gold in the women's 400 metres at the 1994 Commonwealth Games. She also set up the Cathy Freeman Foundation (now known as Community Spirit Foundation) in 2007 to work with four remote Indigenous communities to close the gap in education between Indigenous and non-Indigenous Australian children.

▼ **SOURCE K** Australia's $50 banknote features David Unaipon (1872–1967), a Ngarrindjeri man, preacher, inventor, Indigenous rights advocate and the first Aboriginal writer to be published. The design elements on the banknote reflect aspects of Unaipon's life, such as shields from the Ngarrindjeri nation.

Consequence

Describe two consequences of British colonisation of Australia for Indigenous Australians.

3.5 An independent Australia

The first British colonisers (and convicts) arrived in Australia in 1788. They built their first settlement around a harbour, and this later grew into the city of Sydney. More people arrived and the British took over different parts of Australia over the next few decades. Indigenous Australians were driven from the land that the British took over. By the 1830s, there were lots of different settlements around Australia, and the country itself was divided into four separate colonies – New South Wales, Western Australia, South Australia and the island of Tasmania.

Objectives

- Describe how British colonists gradually gained more freedom from the British government in London to run their own affairs.
- Explain how colonial Australia was governed.

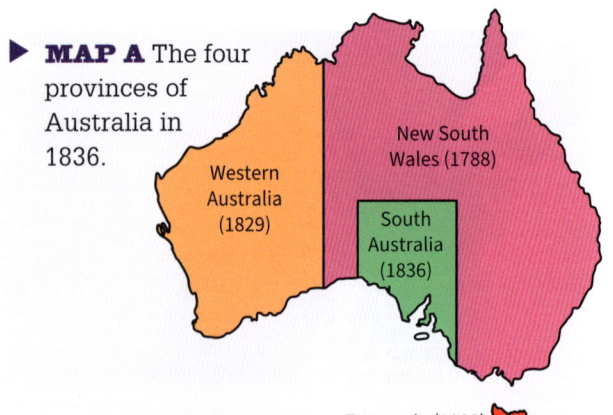

▶ **MAP A** The four provinces of Australia in 1836.

There were special councils in each of the four Australian colonies – with governors in charge – that took some responsibility for running things in the colony. The colonies were all run slightly differently, having different rules and ideas about land, education, the railways, and so on. Of course, Australia was still part of the British Empire, and all the big decisions were made by the British Parliament – but the everyday running of each colony was left to the governor and their council.

However, by 1901 the colonies had united, and Australia was running itself and making key decisions that concerned the whole of the country through its own parliament. So, how did this change happen? This timeline shows how an 'independent Australia' came into being.

1770 Captain Cook arrives in Australia and claims it for the British.
Australia is already home to perhaps 750,000 Indigenous Australians living in around 500 indigenous groups (or 'nations').

1788 First colony built in Sydney Cove.
The Frontier Wars begin at this time.

1790 Free settlers begin to arrive in Australia.
The Frontier Wars intensify.

1803 New colony set up for convicts on Tasmania.
Free settlers soon follow. Tasmania's Indigenous population (around 20,000 people) almost wiped out by settlers.

1840 About half the white population living in Australia were born there.
The Frontier Wars continue.

1851

1855

Chapter 3: Australia

The break from Britain

1901 is a very important year in the history of non-Indigenous Australia. Australia established its own constitution (set of rules by which a country is governed) and controlled the vast majority of its own affairs. It created its own army and navy as well as new laws on education, transport and much more. However, the British monarch remained Head of State – and does to this day. The monarch does not have a role in the day-to-day running of the country and has no real power. Some Australians do not want the British monarch as their Head of State.

Fact ✓

There is no mention of Indigenous Australians in the constitution. As a result, Indigenous Australians aren't protected from racial discrimination by the constitution. A law against racial discrimination was passed in 1975, however laws are more easy to change than the constitution. There is a campaign to update the constitution to recognise Indigenous Australians and protect their rights.

Later on... 1984

For decades, Indigenous Australians were subject to regulations that stopped them having equal voting rights. It was not until 1984 that they were finally treated like other voters.

Over to You

1 a List the four Australian colonies that existed by 1836 and the six that existed by 1859.
  b Describe what sort of things each colony controlled.
  c Why do you think Britain let these areas run certain things themselves?

2 Today, many Australians claim that 1901 marked the 'birth of their nation'. What do you think they mean?

3 Create your own timeline charting the key events in the history of Australia from 'colonisation to independence' (1770–1901).

Gold discovered in Australia even more settlers arrive.
Indigenous population drops rapidly as a result of wars, massacres and diseases introduced by the settlers.

Now over 80 per cent of the white population of Australia were born there. The six colonies meet to draw up a set of rules about how to run as a united country, independent of Britain.

The 'Commonwealth of Australia' is created. The colonies form one 'Federation' with its own parliament. But the British monarch remains Head of State.
The population of Indigenous Australians has declined to about 90,000.

New colony, Victoria, set up.

Queensland, the last colony to be created, comes into existence.

1859   **1890**   **1891**   **1901**

Four of the five Australian colonies granted 'self-government'. They manage most of their own affairs but are still part of the British Empire.

By now all six colonies are 'self-governing'. Indigenous Australian children forcibly taken away (stolen) from their families – the 'Stolen Generations'.

British Empire

3 Have you been learning?

Quick Knowledge Quiz

Choose the correct answer from the three options:

1. Australia's Indigenous peoples are two distinct cultural groups. The Aboriginal peoples live on the islands of Australia and Tasmania. But which group live on the islands in the sea just to the north of Australia?
   a. Torres Strait Islander peoples
   b. Tasman Sea peoples
   c. Collier Bay peoples

2. At the time of the first contact with Europeans, approximately how many Indigenous Australian tribes or nations were there?
   a. 5
   b. 50
   c. 500

3. Indigenous Australians feel a responsibility to protect the natural world, and only take the animals and plants they need. What is this view sometimes called?
   a. Green Agenda
   b. Caring for Country
   c. Eco Care

4. In what year did James Cook first land on the east coast of Australia at Botany Bay?
   a. 1770
   b. 1775
   c. 1780

5. Cook was helped by a brilliant navigator from the island of Tahiti with excellent knowledge of the Pacific Ocean. What was his name?
   a. Tupaia
   b. Endeavour
   c. Gweagal

6. What Latin term, meaning 'land belonging to no one', did the British use to justify the invasion and settlement of Australia?
   a. *terra nullius*
   b. *Terra Australis Incognita*
   c. *terra firma*

7. The British used Australia as a place to send convicted criminals. What was this policy called?
   a. immigration
   b. transportation
   c. retribution

8. Indigenous Australians resisted the arrival of the British. What name was given to the series of conflicts and battles between the Indigenous Australians and the British?
   a. Seven Years War
   b. The Flagstaff Wars
   c. The Frontier Wars

9. Which well-known Indigenous Australian led a series of raids on British settlements from 1792?
   a. Tupaia
   b. Pemulwuy
   c. Yagan

10. In what year did Indigenous Australians gain equal voting rights?
    a. 1901
    b. 1951
    c. 1984

Chapter 3: Australia

Have you been learning?

 Literacy Focus

Note-taking

Note-taking is a vital skill. To do it successfully, you must pick out all the key (important) words and information in a sentence. The key words are the words that are vital to the meaning (and your understanding) of the sentence. For example, in the sentences:

> Australia's Indigenous peoples are two distinct cultural groups but with great diversity within these groups. Aboriginal peoples live on mainland Australia (including Tasmania) – the world's largest island, and a continent in itself. The Torres Strait Islander peoples live on the islands in the sea to the north east of Australia. Both groups of Indigenous Australians adapted their lives to their environment and circumstances'

… the key words are: *two groups Indigenous Australians; diversity within groups; Aboriginal peoples on island of Aus; world's largest island; a continent; Torres Strait Islander peoples on islands in sea to N of Aus.; groups adapted lives to environment and circumstances*

The original sentence was nearly 60 words long – but the shortened version is just over 30 words long and contains abbreviations ('Aus' for 'Australia', and 'N' 'north'). Note-taking like this will help your understanding of events – and provides you with a great revision exercise.

1. Write down the important words in the following sentences. These important words are your notes.
   a. Prior to the arrival of the British, Aboriginal Australians used natural resources for everything they needed – food, shelter, tools, weapons and medicine. Extended family groups consisted of around 25 to 30 people, each with a specific area to hunt in.
   b. Torres Strait Islanders were farmers, who also hunted and fished for food. They are divided into five cultural groups and speak several languages.
   c. Many Aboriginal peoples lived as subsistence hunters, which means they only gathered enough edible plants and killed enough wild animals and fish to meet their needs. Men hunted mainly for larger animals, such as kangaroos, emus and reptiles, while women hunted smaller animals and collected fruits, eggs and plants.
   d. The majority were nomadic too, which means they moved around the countryside to hunt and gather food in tune with the seasons, rather than staying in one place. However, there is evidence that some groups established permanent settlements.
   e. Indigenous Australians have a deep connection to the land, water and all living things. This relationship with the natural world is linked to their belief that everything (humans, animals, rivers, hills, plants, planets, stars and so on) was created by ancient spirits – and these spirits are now part of the landscape, living on in the environment.
   f. As a result, Indigenous Australians feel a responsibility to protect the natural world. This means they only take the animals and plants they need because they want to ensure that natural resources will still be available for future generations. This view is sometimes referred to as 'Caring for Country'.

Vocabulary recall

2. In the anagram list below you will find:
   a. European term for an 'unknown southern land'
   b. Captain Cook's ship
   c. First area named by Cook in Australia
   d. Also known as 'Invasion Day'
   e. Famous Indigenous Australian who resisted the British between 1792 and 1802
   f. Discovered in Australia in 1851
   g. Children taken from their families between the late 1800s and 1969

All the answers are given below, but in the wrong order and with their letters mixed up. Can you unravel them?

- ales snout whew
- astra intercartilaginous
- el umw yup
- alia saturday
- agnesse linnet root
- dogl
- ever douna

British Empire 69

Big Question 6: How did people resist colonisation?

The British spent many years invading and conquering lands all over the world and making them part of the British Empire. But very often these invasions were fiercely resisted by the people whose land the British were taking. Read through the information below carefully – it outlines several instances of the empire fighting back.

Objectives
- Identify places where British colonisation was resisted.
- Outline why different groups and peoples resisted the British.

The Jamaican Maroons

The Maroons were people who had once been enslaved, but fled to mountainous or remote areas, where it was difficult for slave owners to catch them. Here, they formed independent communities as free men and women. In Jamaica, there were a number of Maroon communities who lived in the mountains.

The Jamaican Maroons hunted for food and farmed the land, and occasionally raided British plantations to take food and supplies. They were highly organised and skilled hunters and, as hard as it tried, the British army could not control or defeat them. Eventually, after two exhausting Maroon Wars (1720–1739, 1795–1796), the British made a peace deal with the Maroons that meant they remained free and self-governing.

SOURCE A One of the most famous Maroon leaders of all was named Queen Nanny (1686–1733). She was a skilled fighter who unified different Maroon communities. She is one of Jamaica's official 'National Heroes' and her portrait is on the Jamaican $500 banknote (called 'a Nanny' in Jamaica).

The Anglo-Afghan War

In 1838, a large British army went to Afghanistan (on the north-west border of India) to increase Britain's grip on the area. Britain was concerned that Russia was about to take land in the area – and wanted to control the land itself. Although the British managed to capture the capital (Kabul), and put their own officials in charge, the Afghans fought back ferociously. During the armed resistance, two top British generals were killed and the British decided to leave.

In January 1842, 4,500 British troops, along with 12,000 camp followers (wives, children, servants), marched out of Kabul, hoping to retreat to Jalalabad, around 145km away. However, they soon came under attack from Afghans and the retreat ended in slaughter. Just one man reached Jalalabad, Dr William Brydon. When he arrived, battered and bloody, he was asked, 'Where is the army?' He replied, 'I am the army.'

INTERPRETATION B A painting by Elizabeth Thompson of Dr William Brydon on the retreat from Kabul, called *The Remnants of an Army* (1879).

Big Question

▼ **MAP C** The British Empire in 1921.

The Flagstaff War (or Heke's War)

The Māori are the Indigenous peoples of New Zealand. Their population may have reached as high as 200,000 before Europeans began colonising New Zealand in the 1800s. The European invaders brought diseases which reduced the Māori population further, and a series of wars robbed them of their land.

By 1845, an important Māori leader named Hōne Heke had become increasingly frustrated by the British presence in New Zealand. To show his unhappiness, Hōne Heke chopped down the flagpole (also known as 'flagstaff') at the British settlement of Kororāreka (which had recently been renamed Russell). When the British replaced it, he did it again. And again. After the final felling (in March 1845), a war began between British troops and some northern Māori. Finally, after several bloody battles, a ceasefire was agreed – but the flagpole stayed down.

▶ **INTERPRETATION D**
An artist's impression of Hōne Heke and other Māori chopping down the flagpole.

Fact ✓

Nobody knows for sure where the word 'Maroon' comes from. It might be from an Indigenous Caribbean word meaning wild or from the Spanish 'cimarrones' which means 'people from the mountains'.

Over to You

1 Write a sentence or two to explain who the following were:
   - the Maroons
   - Hōne Heke

2 In your own words explain how different groups fought back against the British in the following areas:
   - Jamaica
   - New Zealand
   - Afghanistan

British Empire

How did people resist colonisation?

The Boxer Rebellion

In 1898, a large secret society formed in China called the Society of Righteous and Harmonious Fists. Members practised Chinese martial arts and felt their skills protected them from bullets. Chinese martial arts were known as 'Chinese boxing' by Europeans – so they became known as the 'Boxers', and their uprising was called the Boxer Rebellion.

The Boxers were mainly poor, Chinese peasants who were fed up with the growing influence of foreign countries in their land. They wanted to expel all foreign people from China. They were unhappy with the British, for example, because they had been selling opium (an addictive drug) in China for years, and when the Chinese objected, war broke out (the Opium Wars). The British defeated the Chinese and took even more land, including Hong Kong, and forced the sale of opium onto the Chinese.

In 1898, the Boxers began to roam China, seizing foreign-owned properties, ripping up railway tracks, and attacking (and sometimes killing) foreign people and any Chinese people who had converted to Christianity. After months of attacks an international army of around 50,000 from Japan, Russia, Britain, France, the United States, Germany, Austria-Hungary and Italy arrived in China and finally defeated the Boxers.

▼ **SOURCE E** A Chinese woodcut from 1899 showing the Boxer Rebellion.

The Irish War of Independence

People from England and Scotland had been settling in and colonising parts of Ireland since the twelfth century. In 1800, British politicians voted that the whole of Ireland should become part of Britain. On 1 January 1801, Great Britain and Ireland officially united to become the United Kingdom of Great Britain and Ireland. Soon all the major decisions about Ireland were being taken by the government in London.

Many Irish people wanted more control over their country. They wanted Ireland to have its own parliament and run itself. These people became known as nationalists (because of their strong desire for an independent nation). However, there were other Irish people who wanted Ireland to stay part of the UK. They were known as unionists (because they supported the 'union' between Ireland and Britain). The unionists lived mainly in the northern part of Ireland, called Ulster.

During the First World War, some Irish nationalists saw a chance to gain independence from the UK. In April 1916, during Easter week, a group of nationalists took control of Dublin (Ireland's capital) and declared independence. The British sent in troops to suppress the uprising and after five days the Easter Rising (as it is known) had been stopped.

▼ **SOURCE F** From the Irish Proclamation of Independence, 1916. This text was read by Padraig Pearse, one of the leaders of the Easter Rising, on the steps of the General Post Office in Dublin.

> 'We declare the right of the people of Ireland to the ownership of Ireland, and to the unfettered control of Irish destinies, to be sovereign and indefeasible… In every generation the Irish people have asserted their right to national freedom and sovereignty; six times during the past three hundred years they have asserted it in arms. Standing on that fundamental right and again asserting it in arms in the face of the world, we hereby proclaim the Irish Republic as a Sovereign Independent State, and we pledge our lives and the lives of our comrades-in-arms to the cause of its freedom, of its welfare, and of its exaltation among the nations.'

SOURCE G The General Post Office, Dublin, in May 1916 after the Easter Rising. The building was used as a headquarters by the rebels during the uprising and was almost completely destroyed by fire caused by British shelling. It reopened in 1929.

MAP H Ireland after it was divided in 1921.

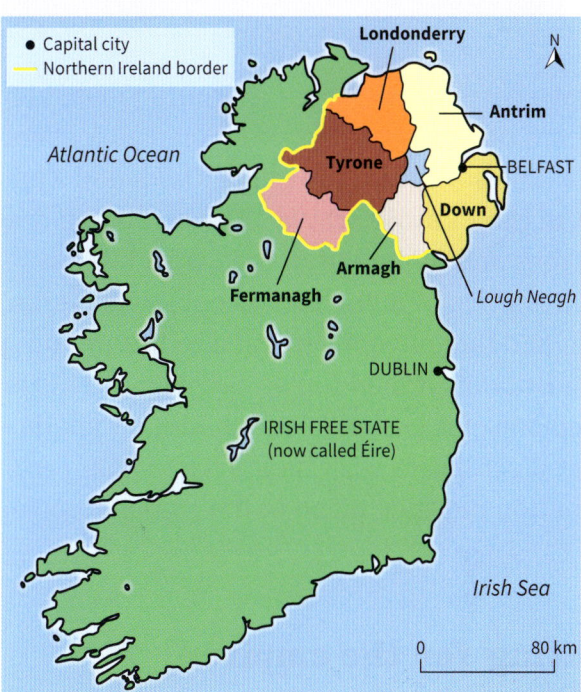

At the time of the Easter Rising, the nationalist rebels had little support, but after 15 of them were executed by the British army, public opinion in Ireland began to change. The Easter Rising rebels were seen by some as national heroes who had died for their beliefs and their country.

In the next few years after the Easter Rising, there was much violence between nationalists and unionists. The unionists were supported by the British government. This period in Irish history is known as the Irish War of Independence or the Anglo-Irish War.

Eventually, in December 1921, a treaty was agreed, ending the war. Six counties in the north of Ireland (where most people were unionists) would remain part of the UK, and be called Northern Ireland. The remaining 26 counties (where the majority were nationalists) would form the Irish Free State, which would run its own affairs, but still remain part of Britain's empire.

The Irish Free State was established in 1922. Now Ireland was divided – and some people were happy, while others weren't. Some felt that all of Ireland should be united, while others thought the split was a sensible compromise. However, the major divisions relating to the split sparked many years of political issues and conflict.

Later on...

The Irish Free State (by then, known as Éire – Irish for 'Ireland') remained neutral during the Second World War. In 1949, it became the fully independent Republic of Ireland and not part of Britain's empire.

Over to You

1. a Who were the Boxers?
   b Why did they resist British rule?
2. a What were the key differences between nationalists and unionists in Ireland?
   b What was the Easter Rising?
   c The Easter Rising is remembered with pride by many Irish people. Do you think it is mainly nationalists or unionists who remember it with pride? Explain your answer.
   d Explain why there are two countries within the island of Ireland.

Consequence

Explain two consequences of the Easter Rising.

Big Question 7: How did the Empire help win two world wars?

Meet two very brave people. So courageous, in fact, that they were both awarded bravery medals for their heroic actions. The soldier on the left is Khudadad Khan and he fought in the First World War. The soldier on the right is Ulric Cross and he fought in the Second World War. Khan and Cross were two of millions of people who weren't born in Britain, and had never even been to Britain, but joined up to fight in Britain's armed forces. So, why did these two people, and millions of other people from India, Canada, Australia and the West Indies, risk their lives to fight for Britain? What contribution did they make to the British forces?

Objectives

- Examine why soldiers from the British Empire fought for Britain.
- Evaluate the impact of the British Empire on the two world wars.

Fighting for the empire

When the First World War broke out in 1914, a great rush of men in Britain volunteered to fight 'for King and country'. There were also lots of volunteers from countries that were part of the British Empire, such as Canada, Australia, New Zealand, India, the West Indies, South Africa and other parts of Africa under British rule. In fact, the British forces would have struggled without them, because when war broke out there were ten times as many German soldiers as there were British.

▲ **SOURCE B** Ulric Cross was born in Trinidad in 1917. He was one of 250 Trinidadians who joined the RAF when war broke out. He flew more than 80 bombing missions, 20 of them over Germany. His plane landed seven times without its wheels because they had been shot away or wouldn't lower.

▶ **SOURCE A** A photograph of Khudadad Khan from a 1915 newspaper. Khan was born in what is now Pakistan. He gained the Victoria Cross in October 1914 after he was wounded, fought off a German attack with his rifle, and managed to get back to the trenches after being left for dead.

Other contributions

During the First World War some empire countries gave food to Britain in case supplies ran short. Canada sent a million bags of flour, about two million kilos of cheese, over a million tins of salmon and 100,000 large bags of potatoes. Some gave money – the West Indian colonies handed over nearly £2 million from taxes and voluntary donations, while India contributed £150 million.

Big Question

▶ **SOURCE C**
A First World War recruitment poster. By autumn 1914, one in every three soldiers fighting for Britain in France was from India.

The ultimate sacrifice

At the end of the First World War, Britain's war dead numbered about 700,000. The total number of dead from around the empire was over 200,000: India lost up to 64,000 soldiers, Australia and New Zealand lost 75,000 and Canada lost 56,000. Colonial troops were involved in some of the bloodiest battles of the entire war – Ypres, the Somme, Gallipoli and Passchendaele. Colonial troops also won hundreds of medals, including over 150 Victoria Crosses – the highest bravery award in the empire.

▼ **INTERPRETATION E** From a 2009 Channel 4 television programme presented by Ian Hislop called *Not Forgotten: 'Soldiers of Empire'*.

'Two and a half million soldiers from the Empire fought in the First World War. They made a vital contribution to the British war effort and to eventual victory. More than a quarter of a million men made the ultimate sacrifice… Before the war, people had referred to the colonies as "dependent" – but during the war, Britain became dependent on them! Without them, without the "soldiers of Empire", the British could not have won.'

How many empire soldiers were there?

Around 2.5 million men from Britain's colonies and dominions fought for Britain during the First World War. It meant that Britain's army contained soldiers from Europe, North America, South America, Australia, Asia and Africa.

For example, over 600,000 Canadians served in the war and Canadian soldiers fought in most major battles. In 1910, Canada's Prime Minister had said, 'When Britain is at war, Canada is at war. There is no difference at all.'

Around 1.4 million people from India volunteered as both soldiers and labourers – the largest volunteer army the world had yet seen. British colonies in Africa provided over 120,000 soldiers, who played a key role in fighting the Germans in Africa, despite facing racial discrimination. In addition, around 15,000 Caribbean soldiers joined up.

▼ **SOURCE D** Soldiers from the Caribbean in 1916. High numbers of casualties meant these troops (who usually had support roles such as cooking and carrying shells) were called to fight. Although called to fight, they didn't get paid as much as white soldiers and were rarely promoted.

Over to You

1. Can you think of reasons why men like Khudadad Khan, Ulric Cross and other people from the British Empire might have joined up to fight?

2. Look at **Source C**. Write a sentence or two explaining:
   a who the 'old lion' and the 'young lions' were
   b who the poster was meant to appeal to
   c how it tried to do this
   d how successful you think it was in getting men to join the British forces.
   e whether you think this poster is inclusive of British colonies in the West Indies and Africa

Source Analysis

1. Read **Interpretation E**. What point is the presenter making about the contribution of the British Empire during the First World War?
2. Do you agree? Give reasons for your answer.

How did the empire help win two world wars?

The Second World War

As in the First World War, the contribution of British Empire nations during the Second World War was huge. While most empire countries were still governed by Britain, some (such as Australia and Canada) were now 'self-governing', so they were not as tied to Britain as before. However, they were still strongly linked to Britain.

Not just the soldiers

But nations did not just contribute to the war effort with soldiers, sailors and aircrew. India, for example, served as a training base and provided vast quantities of food to Britain (some of it was forcibly taken, however). African countries supplied vital raw materials such as rubber, tin, palm oil, steel and cotton. Canada built thousands of tanks, ships and aircraft, while West Indian men and women volunteered to fill jobs in Britain where there was a shortage of workers, such as in factories and on farms. Most empire countries also gave money to Britain to help it fight the war.

▼ **INTERPRETATION F** Adapted from *The Raj at War* by historian Yasmin Khan (2015). The author is discussing the reasons why Indians joined the British army during the Second World War.

'Men entered the army in different ways and for different reasons. Some joined because their families were loyal to Britain and very pro-British. At the other end of the spectrum, others had their arms heavily twisted and felt direct pressure from their landowners or overseers. Service in the army had long been recognised as a way of making sure you received a supply of rice or bread.'

▶ **MAP G** The contribution of British Empire soldiers to the war.

Canada: Just over one million Canadians fought against Italy and Germany in Europe and against Japan in the Pacific region.

Caribbean: About 16,000 Caribbeans volunteered to serve. Over 6,000 served with the RAF as ground staff, fighter pilots, bomb aimers and machine-gunners (including Ulric Cross).

Africa: British colonies in West Africa (The Gambia, Sierra Leone, the Gold Coast (now Ghana) and Nigeria) served as military bases. Thousands of people from British East Africa (Kenya, Uganda, Tanganyika and Zanzibar (now Tanzania)) joined the armed forces, as well as 60,000 from Northern and Southern Rhodesia (now Zambia and Zimbabwe).

India: Over two million Indians fought in the war – the largest volunteer army in history. They fought in Europe, as well as in Sudan against the Italians, in Libya against the Germans and in Burma against the Japanese (among others). Indian troops received over 4,000 medals – including 31 Victoria Crosses.

South Africa: Over 330,000 South Africans fought for Britain in North Africa, East Africa and Madagascar. The South African Air Force made an important contribution in East Africa, North Africa, Sicily, Italy and the Balkans.

Australia: Almost one million Australians served in the war. They fought against Germany and Italy in Europe, the Mediterranean and North Africa, as well as against Japan in Southeast Asia.

New Zealand: Around 160,000 New Zealanders fought on Britain's side in many of the key campaigns in Europe and the Pacific region.

Big Question

INTERPRETATION H From a documentary video produced by the Imperial War Museum in 2022.

'It's definitely a bit of a myth that Britain stood alone during the Second World War. As an island nation Britain absolutely relied on its empire for people, for the land, for the resources, and that is really not always acknowledged... By 1941, Canada had opened 150 new factories to support the war effort... Australia took to building heavy guns. In South Africa, land of gold fields and farmers, they developed a steel industry and produced armoured cars... To produce all of these ships, planes and tanks Britain needed raw materials which again came from across the Empire. Trinidad and Tobago were the Allies' largest producers of oil. Ceylon, which is now Sri Lanka, produced 60 per cent of Allied rubber and Nauru exported one million tons of phosphate annually. Nigeria sent tin, the Gold Coast sent manganese, and Gambia sent ground nuts. Anything you can think of the British Empire was mining, making, or growing it and sending it to Britain.'

SOURCE J Indian soldiers during the Second World War.

Meanwhile... 1939–1945

Britain's Prime Minister during the Second World War, Winston Churchill, has been heavily criticised for diverting vast quantities of food from India to Britain during the war, leading to widespread famine in India which killed up to three million people.

SOURCE I
This poster was issued in Britain in 1941. Its aim was to reassure people that they had allies all across the British Empire.

Over to You

1. Describe the contribution towards the Second World War of countries within the British Empire.

2. Look at **Source I**. Write a sentence or two explaining:
   a. what the poster shows
   b. what the point of the poster is
   c. why you think it was published at that particular time

3. Read **Interpretation F**. What point is the author making about the people from India who joined the British army?

Causation

'Britain would not have won the two world wars without the contribution of the countries within its empire.' How far do you agree with this statement?

4.1 Africa and its kingdoms

Africa is the second largest continent in the world, after Asia, making up about one-fifth of the total land surface of Earth. Today, there are more than 50 independent countries in Africa and on the islands off the African coast. Since ancient times there were large African kingdoms and empires where art, music, poetry and architecture flourished. Goods such as gold, ivory, cloth and salt were traded with distant countries along vast trade routes. Some of these kingdoms and empires were among the richest the world has ever known. However, from the nineteenth century until after the Second World War, most of Africa was invaded and controlled by European countries. Britain and France controlled the most land, but Belgium, Spain, Portugal, Germany and Italy also took over large areas. This chapter looks at why Africa was so appealing to foreign countries, how it was colonised, and how many African nations regained their independence.

Objectives

- Outline key features of the African continent.
- Examine why Africa was targeted by European colonisers.

Amazing Africa

Africa is amazingly varied. It contains dry, hot deserts, vast grasslands, long mountain ranges and tropical jungles. It is surrounded by oceans and seas – the Mediterranean Sea, and the Southern, Atlantic and Indian Oceans. Africa is rich in natural resources – oil, silver, salt, rubber, cotton, copper, coffee, sugar and timber. The continent contains 40 per cent of the world's gold. So, any country that made strong trade links with Africa could become very rich and powerful. Any country that managed to take control of large parts of Africa could become even more so.

▲ **SOURCE A** Sankore Mosque (also called the Sankore University) is one of three ancient centres of learning located in Timbuktu, Mali. It was built during the reign of Mansa Musa (1312–1337).

African kingdoms

Africa has been the centre of some of the world's great civilisations and kingdoms. For example, Ancient Egypt was a society based along the River Nile in North Africa which ruled for over 3,000 years and built the Great Pyramids. In the Middle Ages, large, well-organised trading kingdoms developed in West Africa. The first was the Kingdom of Ghana, which existed from at least the seventh to the thirteenth centuries. The Kingdom grew incredibly rich from trading in copper, gold and ivory along the Niger and Senegal Rivers. The Kingdom of Ghana was followed by the Kingdom of Mali (from the 1200s to the 1600s), and the Kingdom of Songhay, which was most powerful in the 1400s and 1500s. These kingdoms grew wealthy through trade and the collection of taxes on trade.

Later on...

In the late seventh century, Islam spread to North and East Africa. Today, most people in Africa are either Christian or Muslim. In the north of Africa and many West African countries, most people follow Islam, while in central, southern and eastern Africa the Christian faith is generally more common.

Chapter 4: The British in Africa

▶ **MAP B** Africa.

The Great Pyramids: built by the Ancient Egyptians around 4,500 years ago.

The Nile: the longest river in the world, flowing for over 6,600km.

The Sahara: the largest hot desert in the world. It can reach temperatures of 57°C (136°F) in daytime – and below freezing at night.

Mount Kilimanjaro: the highest mountain in Africa at 5,895m. It is located in modern-day Tanzania and is a dormant volcano.

Lake Tanganyika: the world's second deepest lake (after Lake Baikal in Russia). It's nearly a mile deep!

Lake Victoria: bordering Uganda, Tanzania and Kenya, it is the world's second largest freshwater lake (only Lake Superior in North America is bigger).

▶ **SOURCE C** An image from a medieval map showing Emperor Mansa Musa of the Kingdom of Mali. A devout Muslim, Mansa Musa became well known in Europe after his pilgrimage to Makkah in 1324. On the trip, he brought 60,000 people and 80 camels, each loaded with around 140 kilograms of gold. He spent (and gave away) lots of it on the journey. Some historians estimate that Mansa Musa may have been the wealthiest person ever to have lived. His appearance on a map made in Europe shows the European interest in West African trade at this time.

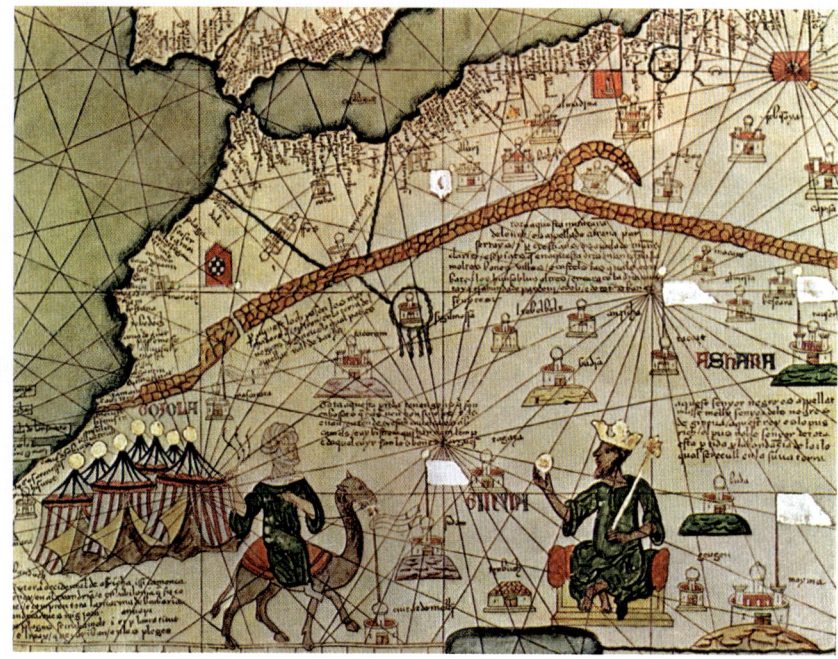

Over to You

1. Write down five facts about the continent of Africa.
2. Look at **Source C**.
   a. Who was Mansa Musa?
   b. What might Mansa Musa's appearance on a European map show us about trade at this time?
3. Suggest a reason why European countries might want to control Africa.

Source Analysis

Give two things you can infer from **Source C** about Mansa Musa.

British Empire

4.2 The invasion of Africa

Until the 1800s, European countries weren't really interested in controlling land in Africa. Instead, they traded with Africa (usually to acquire gold, salt and ivory). They also captured, enslaved and transported people from the west of Africa until 1807 when this trade was banned. Even as late as 1870, just 10 per cent of Africa had been taken over by European countries. Yet by 1900, European nations controlled over 90 per cent of Africa – and Britain was one of the nations that took the most land: 16 colonies were added to the British Empire between 1870 and 1900. Why did this happen?

Objectives

- Explain the origins of the European invasion of Africa in the late 1800s.
- Examine the partition of Africa by European nations.

Why did Europeans want to invade Africa?

- Some of Europe's major nations went 'empire-building' to take (or 'steal') Africa's valuable raw materials such as rubber, cotton, copper, gold and diamonds, and to therefore become richer than their European neighbours.
- Controlling large colonies in Africa was a way to demonstrate power and influence.
- Christian missionaries felt it was their duty to convert Africans to Christianity. They travelled through Africa preaching the benefits of Christianity, and setting up schools and hospitals. Europeans often referred to Africa as the 'dark continent', and missionaries felt it was their role to 'enlighten' it.

The invasion begins

During the 1870s, treatments to combat diseases (like malaria), to which Europeans had no immunity, became available. This increased the pace of European colonisation. After 1880 the rivalry between European nations increased and they raced to grab as much of Africa as they could. This began the partition of Africa, which also became known as the 'scramble for Africa'. To prevent a war erupting between the European powers, their leaders held a conference in Berlin, Germany, during the winter of 1884–1885, to decide which nation could take which areas.

Exploiting Africa

All European powers, including Britain, exploited their colonies. They took their raw materials and used local people as a cheap workforce. Little attempt was made to understand the wishes or needs of the Indigenous peoples, so differences in ethnicity, language, culture and traditions were largely ignored, and the European nations grabbed what they could. Most Africans had little say in how their countries were ruled. In some places, for example Algeria, southern Africa, and Kenya, European settlers took the best land for themselves.

The British invasion

Britain took over 16 huge areas of land (or colonies) in Africa, including Sudan, Nigeria, Kenya, Egypt and Northern and Southern Rhodesia (now Zambia and Zimbabwe). In fact, Britain's land ran in an almost unbroken line from Egypt in the north to South Africa in the south. In total, the British took 32 per cent of Africa by 1900. Control of key areas of land (in southern Africa, for example) was important to the British because it lay along part of the sea route from Britain to India.

▼ **SOURCE A** A well-known African saying. Its origins are unclear but it has been said by both Jomo Kenyatta, independent Kenya's first Prime Minister (1963–1964) and first President (1964–1978), and Archbishop Desmond Tutu, a South African social rights activist.

> 'When the missionaries arrived, the Africans had the land and the missionaries had the Bible. They taught us how to pray with our eyes closed. When we opened them, they had the land and we had the Bible.'

African resistance

African people fought fiercely at times to defend their lands. There were armed rebellions against colonial rule in South West Africa (Herero Revolt, 1904–1907), Eastern Africa (Maji Maji Revolt, 1905–1907) and southern Africa (Bambatha Rebellion, 1906), for example. Sometimes, Africans won major victories over European countries, but often the European invaders wiped out the African forces. After they were defeated, many Africans suffered hardship and hunger as their traditional way of life was destroyed. Some were forced to work as cheap labour in mines or on huge British-owned farms growing tea, coffee, cotton or cocoa for export back to Britain.

Over to You

1. a Why do you think the partition of Africa by European countries in the late 1800s is sometimes referred to as the 'scramble for Africa'?
   b Why do you think Britain was so keen to take part in the partition of Africa?

2. Explain how each of the following contributed to the partition of Africa:
   - political reasons (rivalry between nations)
   - economic reasons (raw materials)
   - religious reasons (Christianity)
   - medical progress

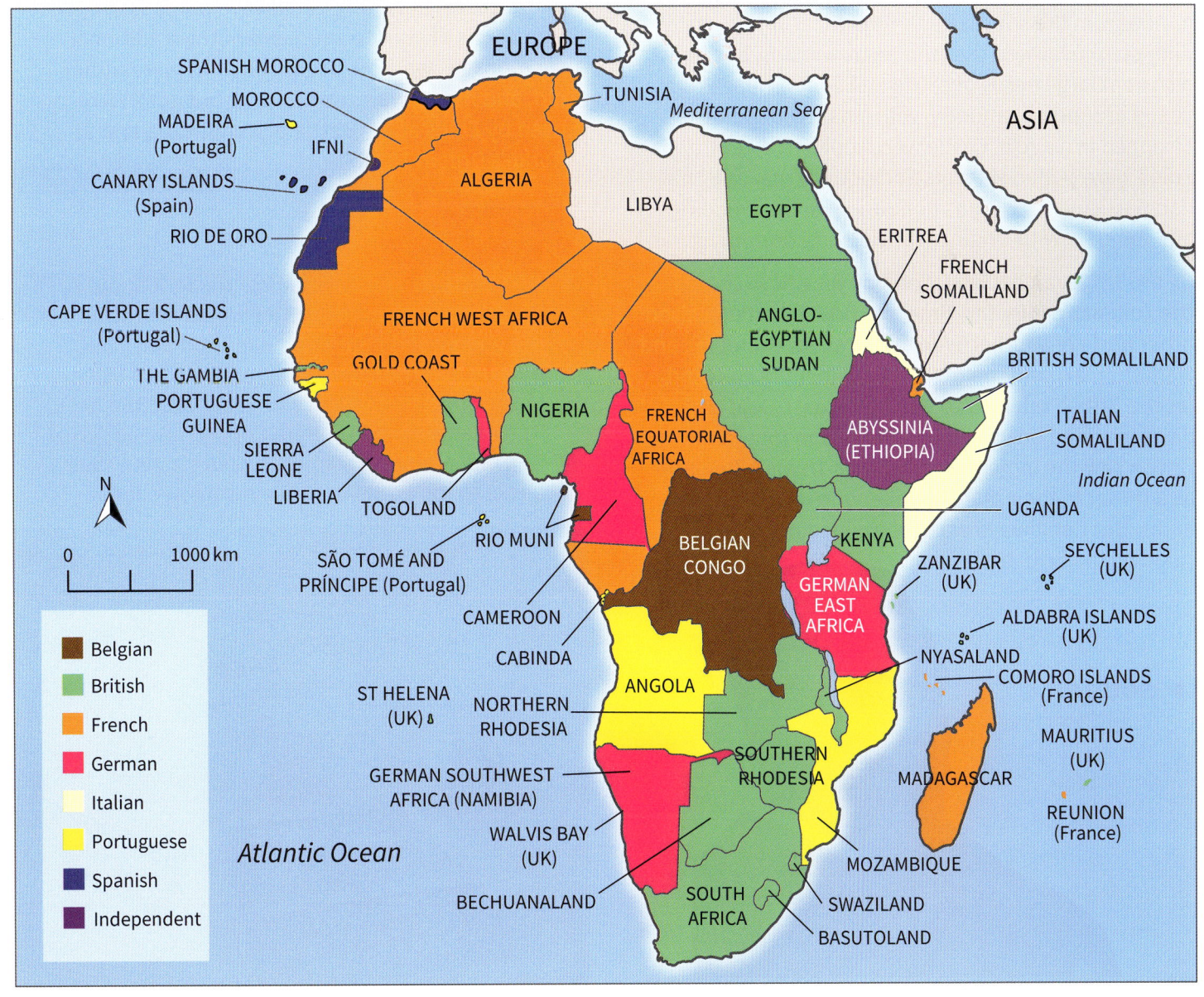

▼ **MAP B** Africa in 1901, showing the areas controlled by various European countries. Almost all of Africa was ruled by seven European nations: Britain, France, Germany, Spain, Portugal, Belgium and Italy.

British Empire

4.3A The Anglo-Zulu War

On Wednesday 22 January 1879 two well-known battles took place just a few miles apart in southern Africa. At the Battle of Isandlwana, a Zulu army took a stand against a British force of 1,300 soldiers and won. Just a short distance away, a group of just 140 British soldiers at a small settlement called Rorke's Drift defended their position against another Zulu army of 5,000 warriors. So, who were the Zulu people? Why were the two sides fighting? What were the consequences of these two battles?

Objectives

- Outline the origins, events and outcomes of the Anglo-Zulu War.
- Examine the tactics and weapons of the Zulu and British armies.
- Assess different sources related to Rorke's Drift.

Who were the Zulu people?

The Zulu people (or Zulus) were an Indigenous group or nation from the southern part of Africa. Traditionally, Zulu people farmed the land to grow crops, but they also kept large herds of cattle and goats. Villages were based around community, with small, round houses arranged in a circle. Cattle were kept in the centre. Many Zulus were skilled weavers and pottery makers. They had particular traditions honouring births, weddings and funerals with singing, dancing and drumming.

By the 1870s, a new king, Cetshwayo, was in charge of the Zulu nation. By this time, the British had colonised other parts of southern Africa (Natal, for example), and wanted to expand their territory to include Zululand (as the British referred to the Zulu areas). Gold and diamonds had been found in the region too – and the British saw the large, powerful, well-trained Zulu army as a threat to their plans to take control of these rich areas. But Cetshwayo was determined not to be ruled by the British.

▶ **SOURCE A** King Cetshwayo during his time in London in 1882.

Fact ✓

In the 1870s, Zulu King Cetshwayo purchased thousands of guns to supplement the traditional weapons his warriors used. The rifles were rather old, and not all warriors had one, but guns were used by Zulus at the Battle of Isandlwana and at Rorke's Drift in 1879.

▼ **SOURCE B** The Zulu 'bull horns formation'. The main force in the centre would charge at the enemy and fight them hand-to-hand. The quickest warriors would move along the sides of the opposition and try to get around the back. The enemy would then be trapped and encircled. The older, reserve soldiers would sit with their backs to the battle until they were needed.

82 Chapter 4: The British in Africa

Key Words: ultimatum

▶ **SOURCE C** A painting of a Zulu village, 1840s. By the early 1800s, there were around 250,000 Zulus. Under King Shaka, they built up an army of around 40,000 soldiers who conquered many of the surrounding Indigenous groups. Their standard tactic was the 'bull horns formation' – a method of fighting that was originally used for hunting but adapted for battle.

▼ **SOURCE D** A painting of a Zulu chief, dressed as a warrior and armed with traditional weapons, 1847.

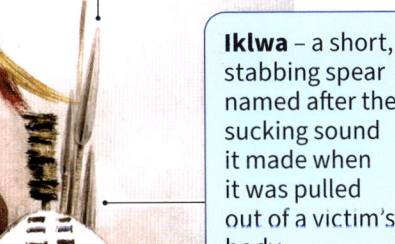

- **Knobkerrie** – type of club.
- **Assegai** – long-bladed spear thrown from a distance.
- **Iklwa** – a short, stabbing spear named after the sucking sound it made when it was pulled out of a victim's body.
- **Cowhide shield** – used to hook the enemy's shield to the side, exposing his ribs for a fatal stab.
- **Bare feet** – Zulus didn't wear shoes but had very tough feet. Warriors could run up to 50 miles a day (nearly two marathons).

The Anglo-Zulu War

In December 1878, the British gave Cetshwayo an **ultimatum**. They told him he had to get rid of the Zulu army, allow British colonisers to move into the area and only make decisions after consulting the British. If he did not agree to this, they would invade. The king gave no reply – so in January 1879 a British army invaded Zululand. The invasion came as a shock to Cetshwayo – he had no desire to fight the British and felt that the relationship (until then) was friendly. The first fighting between Zulus and the British took place on Wednesday 22 January 1879.

British Empire

4.3B The Anglo-Zulu War

1 King Cetshwayo was determined not to be ruled by the British but thought the relationship was friendly. He gave no response to their ultimatum to disband his army and allow the British to invade.

The British army of around 7,000 soldiers marched into Zululand on 11 January 1879.

There were also several thousand local African soldiers fighting with the British. Known as the Natal Native Contingent (NNC), many were from groups that were enemies of the Zulus. The NNC wore their traditional warrior clothing and red bandanas.

The plan was to split the army into three and march towards the royal capital of Zululand – Ulundi.

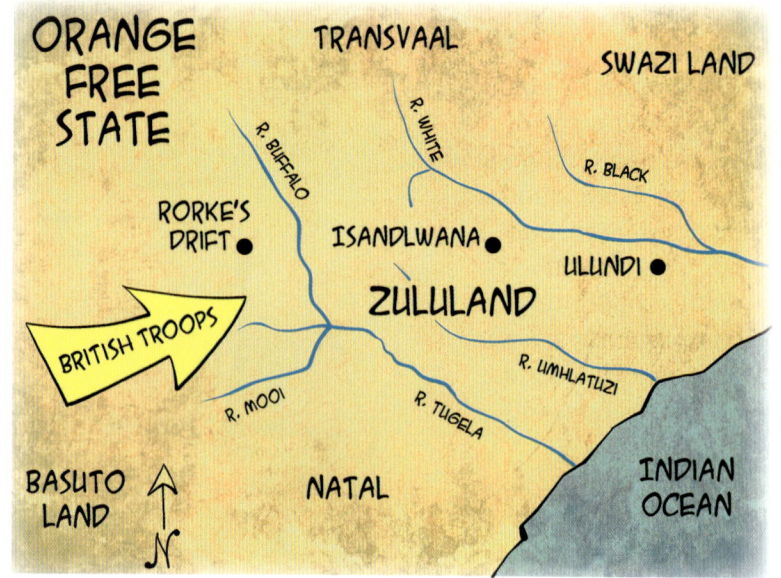

2 The British left a small group of around 140 soldiers and members of the NNC at a former trading post, Rorke's Drift.

Rorke's Drift was to act as a supply depot and medical treatment centre.

3 By 20 January, the main part of the British army got to a hill 16km from Rorke's Drift, called Isandlwana, and set up camp.

After receiving reports that part of the Zulu army was nearby, Lord Chelmsford (the leader of the British army) took two-thirds of the soldiers off to find them at 4:00am on 22 January. The other third stayed behind.

4 The Zulu warriors that had been spotted seem to have been part of a plan by Cetshwayo.

Those few warriors were a decoy. The plan seemed to be to lure lots of British soldiers away from the main camp and leave it poorly defended.

5 With fewer soldiers defending the main camp, over 20,000 Zulus, the main part of Cetshwayo's army, then launched a surprise attack.

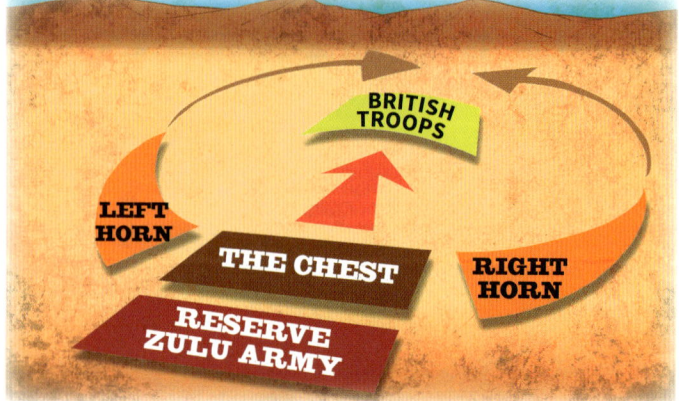

The Zulu army used their traditional 'bull horns formation' to devastating effect.

Chapter 4: The British in Africa

6 Fierce hand-to-hand fighting took place for over four hours.

The majority of the 1,700 British and NNC troops were killed. Supplies and ammunition were also seized.

An estimated 2,000 Zulu warriors were killed.

7 Some British and NNC troops from the camp managed to retreat to Rorke's Drift.

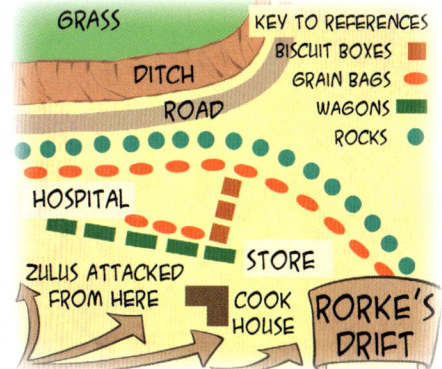

Fearing that the Zulu army would attack there next, they used rocks, wagons, grain bags and even biscuit boxes to build up defences. Only around 120 men were fit enough to fight.

8 A Zulu army attacked Rorke's Drift at around 5:00pm.

There were 4,000–5,000 Zulus in the attack, mainly the reserve warriors who didn't fight at Isandlwana. They again used the 'bull horns formation'.

9 Within two hours the small hospital at Rorke's Drift was on fire and had to be evacuated.

There, 150 British and NNC troops fought off wave after wave of attacks for ten hours before the Zulus retreated.

10 At 8:00am, Lord Chelmsford's army arrived.

In total, 370 Zulus and around 20 British and NNC troops were killed at Rorke's Drift.

11 Eleven Victoria Crosses (VCs) were later awarded to the soldiers of Rorke's Drift. No African NNC soldiers were awarded a VC.

12 The defeat at Isandlwana shocked Britain. The British wrongly believed that, with their more modern weapons, they were superior to the Zulu army. Unsurprisingly, the British newspapers focused on the defence of Rorke's Drift instead.

British Empire 85

4.3c The Anglo-Zulu War

▼ **SOURCE E** Zulu forces won a resounding victory over the British at Isandlwana during the Anglo-Zulu War. Here, King Cetshwayo rallies his warriors on 17 January, a few days before the battle.

'I am sending you out against the whites who have invaded Zululand and driven away our cattle. You are to go against the column at Rorke's Drift and drive it back to Natal… You will attack by daylight as there are enough of you to eat it up, and you will march slowly so as not to tire yourselves…

I have not gone over the seas to look for the white man, yet they have come into my country, and I would not be surprised if they took away our wives and cattle and crops and land. What shall I do? I have nothing against the white man and cannot tell why they come to me. What shall I do?'

▼ **SOURCE G** The memorial to the Zulu warriors who died at the Battle of Isandlwana. The memorial was created in 1999 and is in the shape of a special victory necklace worn by successful Zulu warriors. The necklace is called 'isiqu' or necklace of valour.

▼ **SOURCE H** The site of the Battle of Isandlwana today. The piles of white stones (known as cairns) mark where British soldiers were buried in mass graves.

The aftermath of the battles

Wednesday 22 January 1879 was the day when the British army performed one of its most successful feats (at Rorke's Drift) – yet also suffered one of its most humiliating defeats (at Isandlwana). When news got back to Britain of the events the response was one of both pride and shock. British 'empire-builders' wrongly felt they were superior to Indigenous Africans, who looked different from them and worshipped in a different way. They could not understand how the Zulu army could beat them so convincingly at Isandlwana. It has even been argued that the awarding of 11 Victoria Crosses for the bravery shown by the men of Rorke's Drift was done to take the British public's minds off the defeat at Isandlwana.

▼ **INTERPRETATION F** Professor Saul David, a military historian, novelist and broadcaster, quoted in a 2003 newspaper article.

'Few remember that the battle of Rorke's Drift was fought on the same day that the British Army suffered its most humiliating defeat at nearby Isandlwana. It suited those responsible for the disaster to exaggerate the importance of Rorke's Drift in the hope of reducing the impact of Isandlwana.'

Chapter 4: The British in Africa

The end of the Anglo-Zulu War

The Anglo-Zulu War continued for another six months after the events of 22 January. In March, a Zulu army attacked another British army camp – but was defeated. Finally, the British organised a huge attack on the royal city of Ulundi in July 1879 and the Zulus were defeated. Cetshwayo was captured and sent to London. He was a very popular figure in London and many people were charmed by his polite, friendly manner. He met Queen Victoria and the Prime Minister, and was cheered by crowds when he appeared in public. He returned to southern Africa in 1883 but died shortly afterwards. By then, Zululand had been split into 13 different regions, and was firmly under British control. Yet another part of the world had been absorbed into the British Empire.

▼ **SOURCE I** A painting by Alphonse de Neuville called *The Defence of Rorke's Drift* (1880). The painter visited the battle location shortly after it happened. Note the dog in the painting. The dog (called Pip) belonged to one of the soldiers and played his part in the defence by running along the barricades barking as the enemy approached. Pip survived but his owner didn't. However, Pip was adopted by another soldier and brought back to Britain. Pip is buried with his owner in London's Kensal Green Cemetery.

Over to You

1. Write a narrative account of the events of the Battle of Isandlwana and the defence of Rorke's Drift. You may use the following in your answer:
   - Lord Chelmsford
   - the 'bull horns formation'

   You must also use information of your own.

2. Why might the events of Wednesday 22 January 1879 be viewed differently by British and Zulu people at the time?

3. Look at **Source E**. How useful is this for a historian studying the Anglo-Zulu War?

Source Analysis

1. Look at **Source I**. What impressions do you get of the defence of Rorke's Drift from this picture?

2. How useful is **Source I** for a historian studying the defence of Rorke's Drift?

British Empire

4.4 How did a war in Africa change British schools?

Between 1899 and 1902, the British fought a war in southern Africa called the Second Anglo-Boer War. As a result, the British army needed lots of men to fight. However, around 40 per cent of the men who volunteered were too unhealthy to be soldiers. In some big cities an amazing 90 per cent of men weren't fit enough. This not only worried army leaders, it worried the government too. Within five years of the end of the Second Anglo-Boer War, the government had introduced reforms to make Britain fitter, including free school meals for the poorest children. So, what was the Second Anglo-Boer War all about? Why were so many fit young men needed to fight in it? And how, exactly, did the war lead to free school meals?

Objectives

- Identify why the British fought wars against the Boers in South Africa.
- Examine how an 'empire war' led to fundamental changes in the way Britain cared for its most vulnerable citizens.

Who were the Boers?

In the 1800s, two groups of Europeans competed for control of land in southern Africa – the British and the Boers. The Boers were descendants of Dutch colonisers who had gone to southern Africa in the 1650s. They were mostly farmers ('boer' is the Dutch word for farmer) and their colony was named Cape Colony. In 1806, the British invaded Cape Colony and it soon officially became part of the British Empire. The Boers resented British control and left Cape Colony to head north. They set up two new colonies named the Transvaal and the Orange Free State.

In 1867, diamonds were discovered in the new Boer states. The British sent in troops to try to get the Boers to accept British rule but were beaten back by skilled Boer fighters. This was the First Anglo-Boer War. Then gold was discovered in the 1880s. Thousands of British people arrived, opening dozens of mines. The Boers felt threatened, and their leaders taxed the British miners heavily. During the 1890s, relations between the British and Boers got worse. In 1899 the Second Anglo-Boer War broke out.

The Second Anglo-Boer War

Early on in the war, the small Boer army stunned the British with a series of victories. The British had completely underestimated the Boers, who were highly skilled fighters, armed with modern guns, and knew the terrain well.

▶ **SOURCE A** Boer soldiers mainly fought in groups of 5–12, making them hard to detect. They moved around easily, capturing supplies and attacking troops and communication lines when least expected. They didn't wear uniforms, so they easily blended in with local settlers.

The British fight back

In January 1900, the British responded to their losses by sending half a million troops to fight approximately 50,000 Boer soldiers. The British army used all its hi-tech weaponry – machine guns, modern rifles and high explosive shells. Yet the Boers refused to surrender: after their capital, Pretoria, was captured, they carried on with hit-and-run, 'guerrilla warfare' against British targets.

To isolate their soldiers, Boer civilians were imprisoned in concentration (forced resettlement) camps, where conditions were terrible. Out of 116,000 Boers put in these camps, 28,000 (mainly children) died, largely from disease and illness caused by terrible conditions. About 130,000 Black civilians were also forcibly moved to camps, mostly labourers on Boer farms – and it is thought that at least 20,000 died.

Peace at last

By 1902, both sides were exhausted after years of brutal fighting. Eventually the Boers were forced to surrender, and peace talks began. It was agreed that the Boer states would become British colonies, but the Boers were promised that they could make many of the key decisions in running their lands. It is important to remember that the Anglo-Boer Wars were a conflict between two sets of colonists. The Indigenous peoples in Africa were ignored as the colonists drew up new borders that split the local people into new countries that didn't represent them or reflect their history and customs. In 1910, the Boer states joined with Cape Colony and Natal to form the Union of South Africa, part of the British Empire. However, this Union (commonly known as South Africa) was classed as a dominion, rather than a colony, and ran its own affairs.

Consequences of the Second Anglo-Boer War (1899–1902)

At first, there was plenty of support in Britain for the war and thousands of men volunteered to fight, but this did not last long. Around 450,000 British soldiers fought in the war, and nearly 6,000 died in battle while 16,000 died from illness and wounds sustained in battle. The Boers lost around 7,000 soldiers and over 28,000 civilians. The war showed how determined the British were to hold onto their empire – at whatever cost.

The war also had an unexpected consequence. Young British men had volunteered to fight in their thousands, but over a third were classed as 'unfit for duty'. This worried the government. Unless something was done, how was Britain going to fight its wars in the future?

In 1906, the government decided to act, introducing free school meals for the poorest children. Other measures over the next five years included free medical checks and health treatments in schools. The government also encouraged the teaching of 'domestic science' in schools, which was the study of nutrition, food, clothing, child development, family relationships and household skills. This was a direct result of the fact that so many young people who volunteered to fight in the Second Anglo-Boer War were physically unfit for military service.

The government then moved on to other sections of society, introducing unemployment benefit (the 'dole'), sickness pay and old age pensions. They even built Britain's first job centres. Indeed, it seems that a distant war in southern Africa led to many of the ideas that still help the most vulnerable people in society today.

Key Words guerrilla warfare

▼ **SOURCE B** An illustration from French newspaper *Le Petit Parisien* from January 1901, showing Boer prisoners in a British camp in the Transvaal. The British soldiers are in white helmets.

Over to You

1. Explain the following terms:
   a. Boer
   b. concentration camp
   c. Union of South Africa
2. In your own words, explain how the Second Anglo-Boer War led to improvements for ordinary people in Britain.

Causation

Explain two causes of the Second Boer War.

4.5A Independence in Africa

In the early 1920s, Britain had the largest empire the world. It contained around 450 million people (approximately a quarter of the world's population) and covered about a quarter of total global land area. In Africa, Britain controlled 16 colonies, including Egypt, Sudan, Nigeria, British East Africa (Kenya, Uganda, Tanganyika and Zanzibar), Sierra Leone and South Africa. However, over the next 60 years, each of these colonies became independent from Britain. How and why did this happen?

Objectives

- Evaluate the impact of the First and Second World Wars on the decline of the British Empire in Africa.
- Explain how African nations regained their independence during the twentieth century.

The impact of the world wars

Before the First World War, Britain was one of the world's richest countries, due to its industrial power and vast empire. However, after four years of fighting, this had changed: Britain was now in debt because it had borrowed money (mainly from the USA).

Also, between 1914 and 1918, Britain had not been trading with lots of other countries because it had been concentrating on trying to win the war. As a result, these other countries had found new nations to trade with, or had developed their own industries. In short, the First World War changed Britain's global status – it was no longer the world's economic superpower.

After the war, Britain recovered some of its economic strength, but it was then completely bankrupted by the Second World War. Britain was in more debt than ever before – and needed more loans to recover. This was also the time when the USA and the USSR became world superpowers. Britain was no longer as important as it had been on the world stage.

Leaving the empire

By the end of the war, some of Britain's colonies had been running their own affairs for years. Australia, for example, had been part of the British Empire since 1770, but by 1901 it had its own parliament that made most of the key decisions. New Zealand became a British colony in 1840, but had started to run its own affairs by 1907. South Africa had been self-governing since 1910 and Egypt since 1922. More and more colonies were now demanding the right to govern themselves.

The Second World War had weakened countries like Britain and France, which no longer had the power or wealth to hold on to their colonies. In addition, many African people (living under British and French rule) had fought for Britain and France against Germany,

▶ **MAP A**
The British Empire at its territorial peak in 1921.

defending democracy and freedom, while their own countries were not free or democratic. Seeing this injustice, lots of people living under colonial rule began to demand their own right to democracy and freedom. They wanted to elect their own leaders independently and choose their own governments.

African independence movements

In the 1920s, an independence campaign began in West Africa. A group of West Africans created the National Congress of British West Africa (see Fact box) and asked the British government for more control over their own affairs, but the request was rejected. In Kenya, several groups also formed to fight for self-rule in the 1940s. Indeed, by the end of the Second World War there were large independence movements in several African nations including Nigeria, the Gold Coast, Sierra Leone and The Gambia.

Indian example

When India gained independence from Britain in 1947, many other countries began to demand their freedom. The British decided to allow independence in colonies they considered stable enough. They hoped that by freely granting independence, they were more likely to have a successful relationship with the newly independent countries.

> ### Fact ✓
> Founded around 1917, the National Congress of British West Africa was one of the earliest independence organisations in West Africa. Its founding members (mostly from the Gold Coast), pictured below, included Thomas Hutton-Mills Sr, J.E. Casely Hayford (both lawyers) and Edward Francis Small (a teacher and missionary).

The Gold Coast becomes Ghana

The Gold Coast (its name under British rule) was one of the most stable and prosperous countries in West Africa. In 1947–1948 Gold Coast soldiers who had fought for Britain in the war took to the streets to protest against poverty and lack of benefits for ex-soldiers. In February 1948, the British fired on the peaceful demonstrators and riots followed. Several key political leaders were jailed, including Dr Kwame Nkrumah. In 1949, Nkrumah formed the Convention People's Party (CPP), whose slogan was 'Self Government Now'. The CPP used strikes and boycotts to fight for their aims. Nkrumah was jailed again and in the 1951 elections, Nkrumah won, even though he was still in jail. The British let him out of prison and allowed him to become Prime Minister – but the Gold Coast remained part of the Empire. In 1956, he was re-elected, and the British took this as a sign that they should leave. The Gold Coast became the independent state of Ghana in March 1957.

After Ghana, several other British colonies in Africa quickly became independent. **Chart F** (page 93) shows the speed at which independence was gained throughout Africa, not just in British colonies, but in other European countries' colonies too. However, the switch to independence caused riots and severe violence in some places.

▶ **SOURCE C**
Dr Kwame Nkrumah and Queen Elizabeth II at a ball in Accra, Ghana, in 1961.

▶ **SOURCE B**
Some of the founding members of the National Congress of British West Africa.

> ### Over to You
> 1. Describe the size and scale of the British Empire in the 1920s.
> 2. What impact did the First World War have on the British Empire?
> 3. Why were there more demands for independence in Ghana after the Second World War?

4.5B Independence in Africa

Independence in Kenya

In the early twentieth century European farmers began to settle in Kenya, in East Africa. In 1920, Kenya formally became a British colony. The British government then introduced laws that benefited the white farmers, but pushed Indigenous people from their lands. The group particularly affected by this were the Kikuyu people who farmed in the central highlands.

A number of groups formed to fight for self-rule in the 1940s. One group, the Kenya African Union (KAU) and its leader Jomo Kenyatta, campaigned for both independence and access to white-owned land. Another group, known as the Mau Mau, favoured violence against the white settlers who controlled large areas of land.

The Mau Mau Rebellion

The Mau Mau were mainly young Kikuyu people, who were angry at the loss of their land and lack of political rights. In the early 1950s, they began to attack white settlers and Kikuyu people who were loyal to the British government. The Mau Mau were poorly armed (often using home-made guns and swords) but attacked in small groups so were hard to detect and moved around easily.

Not all Kikuyu people supported the Mau Mau, and when the British government offered protection from the Mau Mau and land reform, many Kikuyu fought with the British against the Mau Mau.

The British campaign against the Mau Mau was extremely violent and thousands were killed. Suspected rebels were put in prison camps, where conditions were terrible. Some suspects were tortured or killed. When news of these atrocities was reported in the British press there was an outcry. Many Kenyan independence leaders (including those unconnected to the Mau Mau, such as Kenyatta) were arrested and jailed. Many white settlers later chose to leave Kenya.

▶ **SOURCE D** A home-made pistol used by Mau Mau fighters during the rebellion.

▶ **SOURCE E** A statue of the Mau Mau leader Dedan Kimathi in Nairobi, Kenya, put up in 2007. The first two Presidents of independent Kenya did not support the Mau Mau, but many Kenyans have now begun to recognise the part the group played in gaining independence.

End of the Rebellion

The Mau Mau Rebellion, as it was known, lasted for over eight years. In total, 32 white settlers were killed, and at least 11,000 Africans (but some historians put the estimates much higher). The British eventually realised that reforms were necessary. In 1957, Indigenous Kenyans were granted the vote. The British government also introduced land reforms designed to reward Kenyans who had been loyal to it, and punish those who had fought with the Mau Mau. This caused long-term problems and left around a third of Kikuyu people without land.

On 12 December 1963, Kenya was granted independence, and Kenyatta, who had been released from prison in 1961, became Prime Minister.

In 2013, Kenyan survivors of torture won a legal case against the British government over abuses committed during the Mau Mau Rebellion. In response, the government apologised for torture and ill-treatment, and agreed to pay compensation.

> **Fact**
>
> Countries with a majority white population were usually granted independence before countries with a mostly non-white population. Racist views at the time meant the British government believed that white people were better able to run a country successfully, which would benefit the Empire as a whole.

▼ **CHART F** Some of the African nations that achieved independence in the 1960s and 1970s.

Flag	Country	Ruler	Date of independence
	Ghana (formerly the Gold Coast)	Britain	1957
	Congo	France	1960
	Mauritania	France	1960
	Nigeria	Britain	1960
	Senegal	France	1960
	Algeria	France	1962
	Uganda	Britain	1962
	Kenya	Britain	1963
	Angola	Portugal	1975
	Mozambique	Portugal	1975
	Zimbabwe (formerly Rhodesia)	Britain	1980

Independent Africa

For many newly independent nations, freedom brought difficulties as well as benefits. Some nations, like Morocco, Tunisia and Egypt, developed successful tourist industries, while others have made use of raw materials such as rubber, gold and diamonds despite these resources having been so depleted by previous centuries of colonial exploitation. Many African nations have developed fast-paced economies with vibrant cities and culture. However, the impact of European colonialism has resulted in ongoing problems in many independent African nations. In some countries, rivalries between ethnic groups have escalated into bloody civil wars. This happened in Nigeria in the 1960s, Uganda in the 1980s, and Sierra Leone, Rwanda and Somalia in the 1990s. Many nations have struggled to create their own systems of government, build up industry and trade, and cope with differences between groups of people. However, perhaps the greatest problem they have had to deal with is poverty.

▼ **INTERPRETATION H** Adapted from a 2016 newspaper article by Professor David Olusoga, a historian of the British Empire.

'The empire did bring economic developments and peace to some parts of the world, though many of those developments did not last and were mainly arranged to suit British interests. And it delivered war and devastation to other regions.'

▶ **SOURCE G** The city of Cape Town in South Africa. The city is known for its natural setting, its harbour, and for well-known landmarks such as Table Mountain (the flat mountain in the background). The stadium in the centre of the photograph was built for the 2010 men's FIFA World Cup – the first time this competition was held in Africa.

Over to You

1. Look at **Source D**. What can you infer about the Mau Mau Rebellion from this source?
2. Describe some challenges many African nations have faced since independence.

Consequence

Describe two consequences of the Mau Mau Rebellion in Kenya.

British Empire

4 Have you been learning?

🔄 Quick Knowledge Quiz

Choose the correct answer from the three options:

1. Which of the following were important African trading empires or kingdoms in the Middle Ages?
   a Mali and Songhay
   b Egypt and Songhay
   c Ghana and Maya

2. What was the name of the emperor of the Kingdom of Mali, said to be the wealthiest person ever to have lived?
   a Sankoré Madrasa
   b Jomo Kenyatta
   c Mansa Musa

3. In 1884–1885, a conference of European leaders took place to decide which nation could take which areas of Africa. Where was it held?
   a Berlin, Germany
   b London, UK
   c Paris, France

4. Which of the following areas of land in Africa became part of the British Empire?
   a Egypt, Algeria and Liberia
   b Nigeria, Kenya and Egypt
   c Kenya, Morocco and Egypt

5. Who led Zulu forces at the Battle of Isandlwana in the Anglo-Zulu War?
   a Shaka
   b Assegai
   c Cetshwayo

6. What was the name of the standard military tactic used by Zulu warriors?
   a bull horns formation
   b creeping barrage
   c guerrilla warfare

7. Who were the Boers?
   a descendants of Dutch colonisers who had gone to southern Africa in the 1650s
   b an Indigenous group of Africans who had migrated from northern Africa
   c British army leaders who worked in southern Africa

8. The Gold Coast (as it was known under British rule) was the first British colony in Africa to become independent. By what name is this country now known?
   a Egypt   b Togo   c Ghana

9. In 2013, the British government apologised for the way it had dealt with which rebellion in Kenya?
   a Mau Mau Rebellion
   b Rorke's Drift Revolt
   c Paika Rebellion

10. Kenya gained its independence from Britain in what year?
    a 1957   b 1960   c 1963

94   Chapter 4: The British in Africa

Have you been learning?

 **Literacy Focus**

Spelling, punctuation and grammar

1. The sentences below don't make much sense. Some words are misspelled, and some sentences need capital letters, full stops and apostrophes.

   Copy out each sentence, correcting capitalisation, spelling, punctuation and grammar as you write.

   a Africa was the center of some of the worlds great civilisations kingdoms and empires for example, Ancient egypt (or the Egyption Empire), was a soceity based along the River nile in northern africa witch ruled for over 3,000 years and built the Great Pyramids

   b In the Middle Ages, large, well-organised trading empires or kingdoms developed in the west of africa. The first was the ghana Empire what existed from at least the seventh to the thirteenth centuries. The empire grew incredibly rich trading in copper gold and ivory along the Niger and Senegal Rivers.

   c The Ghana Empire was followed by the Kingdom of Marlee (from the 1200s to the 1600s), and the Kingdom of Songhay, which was most powerfull in the 1400s and 1500s. These kingdoms grew wealthy threw trade, and the collection of taxs on trade.

   d mansa musa, an emperer of the Kingdom of Mali, become well known in europe after his pilgrimage to Makkah in 1324. On the trip, he brung as many as 60,000 people and 80 camels, each loaded with around 140kg of gold.

   e He spent (and gave away) lots of gold on the journey. Some historians estamate that Mansa Musa may have been the wealthyist person what ever lived.

Chronology

2. The ability to put events in the correct chronological order is vital in history. As you know, history is full of amazing stories – and to understand a story you must know the order in which things happened.

   Put the following events (a–i) in the correct chronological order so you can understand the 'big picture' of the colonisation of Africa:

   a Between 1562 and 1807, British ships took around three million Africans into slavery in America and the Caribbean.

   b The Second Anglo-Boer War, which ended in 1902, saw the Boer states become British colonies, but the Boers were promised that they could make many of the key decisions in running the land.

   c The Ghana Empire existed from at least the seventh to the thirteenth centuries, followed by the Kingdom of Mali and the Kingdom of Songhay.

   d After the Anglo-Zulu War of 1879, Zululand was split up into regions and was absorbed into the British Empire.

   e The Gold Coast (as it was known under British rule) became the independent state of Ghana in March 1957.

   f Between 1880 and 1900, European countries raced to grab as much of Africa for themselves as they could. This became known as the 'scramble for Africa'.

   g Ancient Egypt (or the Egyptian Empire), based along the River Nile in northern Africa, ruled for over 3,000 years.

   h After Ghana, several other British colonies in Africa quickly became independent. The last British colony to become independent was Zimbabwe in 1980.

   i Founded around 1917, the National Congress of British West Africa was one of the earliest independence organisations in West Africa.

British Empire

Big Question 8: How and why have views on the British Empire changed?

Cecil Rhodes was a well-known 'empire-builder'. After his death in 1902, many streets, schools and other buildings were named after him. Statues were built in many colonies to honour him. Zimbabwe, when it was still a British colony, was named Rhodesia after him. However, in 2015, a Cecil Rhodes statue was removed from the University of Cape Town in South Africa (see **Source A**). There are calls for other statues of him to be removed, including one at Oriel College, Oxford, and places renamed. Why have opinions of Rhodes changed over the years? Why is he such a controversial figure today? How and why have views on the British Empire changed?

Objectives
- Examine why Cecil Rhodes has attracted both admiration and hatred.
- Assess how and why views on the British Empire have changed.

Who was Cecil Rhodes?

Born in 1853, Rhodes was both a businessman and a politician. From the 1870s, he became very wealthy working in (and controlling) lots of gold and diamond mines in southern Africa. He then used his money and political skills to gain control of more land. When he died, he left money to many institutions, including the University of Cape Town and Oxford University, which benefited from his generosity. However, Rhodes had racist views and believed that Britain was superior to other countries and their people. He introduced laws that pushed Indigenous Africans from their lands and increased taxes on their homes.

Some have argued that Rhodes was a man 'of his time' and that we shouldn't judge his actions and beliefs by today's standards. Beliefs like the ones held by Rhodes were widely accepted by many people at the time, and that Rhodes was doing what lots of people and countries were doing.

However, even at the time not all British people accepted Rhodes' views. When he died, the *Manchester Guardian* newspaper wrote, 'The judgement of history will, we fear, be that he did more than any Englishman of his time to lower the reputation and to impair the strength and compromise the future of the empire.'

Others argue that there should be no excuse for a person's actions and beliefs, no matter when they lived. Many look at Rhodes differently today because we have different views about empire and race to those that were common in previous centuries.

Generally, statues celebrate a person's life and achievements – but it is argued that the life and achievements of Rhodes should no longer be celebrated.

▶ **SOURCE A** The removal of the Cecil Rhodes statue, in April 2015, from the University of Cape Town. Some people have suggested another solution relating to statues – that they shouldn't be removed but new plaques could be added explaining why the person is controversial.

▶ **SOURCE B** This cartoon appeared in *Punch* magazine in 1892, next to an article about Rhodes' plan to extend an electrical telegraph line from Cape Town in Cape Colony in the south of Africa to Egypt's capital Cairo in the north. Both Cape Colony and Egypt were under British control.

▼ **INTERPRETATION C** Adapted from an article called 'Cecil Rhodes' colonial legacy must fall – not his statue', which appeared in *The Guardian* in March 2015. It was written by Siya Mnyanda, a politics and philosophy graduate from the University of Cape Town (UCT).

'Dr Max Price, vice chancellor of UCT, summed up the contradictions by saying that although Rhodes was considered a "great man", the attitudes and means he used "were not right". [Price said] "He was racist. He used power and money to oppress others. So on balance he was a villain." But as a black former UCT student, who walked past that statue for four years, I think Rhodes should be left exactly where he is. Removing him omits an essential part of the university's history that has contributed to everything good, bad and ugly about it – and arguably the country too.'

Changing views

The British Empire spanned over 400 years and brought vast changes to countries, societies, cultures and people's lives all over the world. In the past, many (but not all) British people viewed the empire as something to be proud of. They tended to think that it was positive that the empire brought trading benefits to Britain and made the country richer. There was also the belief the British had a 'right' to the land and were helping people in conquered nations by teaching them a new, Christian way of life.

Big Question

There was an incorrect racist belief at the time that Christianity and white skin were 'superior' to other religions and skin colours. Queen Victoria said that one of the aims of the British Empire was to 'protect the poor natives and to advance civilisation'. This was a time when most people were very loyal to their monarch and their country, and patriotic pride was encouraged.

However, those attitudes are not common in modern Britain. In recent years, there has been an understanding that the power and wealth that Britain gained from the empire came at a cost to the Indigenous peoples whose lands Britain invaded. It is now acknowledged that many Indigenous people in the colonies – India and Australia, for example – became poorer at the expense of making Britain richer. Much of the work relating to the British Empire today tries to understand the empire from the point of view of the colonised countries.

Over to You

1 Look at **Source A**.
   a Who was Cecil Rhodes?
   b What is happening in the photograph?
   c Briefly outline the debate over the removal of some statues.
   d Do you think the University of Cape Town students were right to vote for the removal of the statue? Discuss with a partner, and give reasons for your answer.

2 How have attitudes about the British Empire changed among some people?

3 Read **Interpretation C**.
   a Describe the two views of Rhodes that Dr Max Price describes.
   b Why does the writer of the article think the statue of Rhodes should stay?
   c Why do you think there are different views of Cecil Rhodes?

Source Analysis

How useful is **Source B** to a historian studying the aims of Britain in Africa?

Big Question 9: What is the legacy of the British Empire?

The British Empire no longer exists. After the Second World War, it began to break apart as lots of colonies gained independence. Today, little remains of British rule across the world. A few areas of land are still officially, politically linked to Britain, but they are mainly small islands such as Bermuda and the Falkland Islands. These are called British Overseas Territories. However, the **legacy** of the British Empire remains. What does this mean?

Objectives
- Define the word 'legacy'.
- Examine the legacy of the British Empire.

What is 'legacy'?

When we talk about 'legacy', it commonly means what someone or something is remembered for, or what they leave behind. It is something that is a part of history that remains from an earlier time. The legacy of the British Empire is complex. It is important to remember, however, that our understanding of what a legacy is can change. New ideas and new ways of thinking mean we can interpret the past differently.

▼ **SOURCE A** Men, women and children from the Caribbean arriving in Southampton in 1962. After the Second World War there were not enough workers in Britain. The government encouraged people to move to Britain from the empire to help rebuild the country.

A legacy of movement

The British Empire caused the mass movement of large groups of people, who made a lasting impact on the areas they moved to. Some of these groups moved voluntarily out of Britain to settle in places such as North America and Australia, while others were taken by force, such as the three million Africans enslaved and transported to British colonies in North America and the Caribbean between 1562 and 1807.

Groups of people from the empire also moved to Britain. For example, in 1948, the British Parliament passed the British Nationality Act. This meant that all the people of the empire – now called the Commonwealth – had British citizenship, which meant they could have a British passport and move to Britain. Between 1948 and 1970, nearly 500,000 people from the Caribbean settled in Britain, for example. They are known as the 'Windrush Generation', named after one of the first ships that brought them from the Caribbean in 1948. In fact, people from all parts of the empire, from Africa, Asia and other places, have settled in Britain – all helping to create a more multicultural country.

Later on... 2017

In late 2017, some of the 'Windrush generation' were told that they were in Britain illegally because they didn't have official paperwork (such as a UK passport). Some were sent back to the Caribbean. Others lost their jobs, or were stopped from having free medical care. This became known as the 'Windrush Scandal'. In August 2018, the British government admitted its mistakes and said that anyone who had left the UK would be helped to return.

Many Asian people from Kenya and Uganda came to Britain in the 1960s and 1970s. They had moved to Africa from India and Pakistan when these nations were part of the British Empire – but now the newly independent Kenyan and Ugandan governments were driving them out. Around 44,000 Asians from Kenya and 26,000 from Uganda came to Britain at this time.

In the 1950s and 1960s, many people came to Britain from the British colony of Hong Kong. By 1961, there were around 30,000 people from this region living in Britain. In 1997, Hong Kong stopped being a British colony and became part of China. Around 50,000 people from Hong Kong were given British passports at this time.

Legacy on the land

The British drew up new borders and land boundaries that split Indigenous peoples into new countries and territories. Some of these borders (in countries such as India, Pakistan, Nigeria and Sudan) are still a source of conflict today. For example, the 2,600km-long Durand Line separating Pakistan from Afghanistan, created by the British in 1893, causes heated international arguments today.

▼ **SOURCE B** A Pakistani soldier at the border between Pakistan and Afghanistan.

Key Words legacy

A legacy of conquest

The power and wealth Britain gained came at a price. Indigenous peoples were taken advantage of by traders and robbed of their land and raw materials. Beliefs, languages and customs of Indigenous populations were sometimes replaced by those of the invaders, which removed their cultural identities and heritage.

Physical legacy

The British built things in the colonies – schools, universities, hospitals, roads and railways. In India, for example, the British built nearly 80,000km of roads and dug nearly 12,000km of canals by 1900. These were built to make it easier to move goods for trade, and to transport soldiers, not for the benefit of the Indian people – but many of these roads and canals remain in India today.

There is also a legacy of empire in some of the things built in Britain. The Royal Pavilion in Brighton, built in the late 1700s and early 1800s, has domes and minarets that echo the style of nineteenth-century Indian buildings.

▼ **SOURCE C** The Royal Pavilion in Brighton was built between 1787 and 1822. It was the seaside home of the Prince of Wales, later King George IV.

What is the legacy of the British Empire?

A sporting legacy

Organised ball games – like football, rugby and cricket – became very popular in Britain in the 1800s. When British people went out to live in the colonies, they took their love of these sports with them. As a result, some of them became very popular in empire countries. Snooker, for example, was invented by British army officers stationed in India, and the top cricketing nations today are all former colonies of the British Empire.

▼ **SOURCE D** England players during the 2022 cricket final against Pakistan. Left to right, the photo shows Chris Jordan (born in Barbados), Ben Stokes (born in New Zealand) and Adil Rashid (born in England of Pakistani heritage).

Legal legacy

Most places had sophisticated systems of law and order before the British arrived. However, British law systems replaced them in many cases.

'Common Law' is the idea that laws are based on decisions made by judges and courts in the past (known as 'precedent'). So, when a court makes a decision about something, that decision becomes a part of the law of the country. In the UK, there is also the idea that people on trial are 'innocent until proven guilty' and have the right to a fair trial. Common Law systems are used in many former colonies of the British Empire, including the USA, India, Canada and New Zealand.

Environmental impact

There was an impact on the natural world. Some animal species were nearly wiped out through hunting (elephants and tigers, for example) and natural habitats were cleared to make way for plantations and farmland. Sometimes, native plants were wiped out because 'English' plants, birds, fish and cattle were introduced.

Legacy of language

When a nation became part of the British Empire, the British made sure that English became the language used there in all trading, industry and business. As a result, English became (and remains) one of the most commonly used languages in dozens of former empire countries, including the USA, Australia, New Zealand, Jamaica, Nigeria, Kenya, South Africa and India. In other places this has caused a decline in the use of Indigenous languages, some have been lost altogether.

Words that were used across the empire made their way into everyday use back in Britain, and are still used today. They had either been heard by British people who had lived abroad, or were brought here by people from the empire who settled in Britain.

Place of origin	Words used in everyday English
India	pyjamas, bungalow, cot, bangle, loot, pundit, shampoo, sentry, chutney, khaki
Africa	banjo, cola, bongo, banana, jazz, zombie, trek, safari
Australia	boomerang, kangaroo, koala
Indigenous America	igloo, kayak, husky, toboggan, pecan, squash, avocado, tobacco, barbecue, hurricane, anorak, cougar, cashew, piranha

Legacy of identity

For centuries, many people in Europe held racist views that Christianity and white skin were 'superior' to other religions and skin colours. Many British people believed that invading other places was the right thing to do because they were bringing 'order' to non-white countries by introducing British ideas and systems.

It has been argued that this has had a deep and long-lasting impact on the way some white people think about themselves. Some people have developed strong ideas about race and think that humans are ranked in order of importance – and that white people are at the top of the list. This is '**white supremacy**'.

▼ **INTERPRETATION E** Adapted from an interview with author and journalist Sathnam Sanghera in *History Extra* magazine, 2021.

'I'd argue that we have a very particular brand of racism in Britain which can be best explained by the white supremacy of empire in the 19th century. The ways that imperialists of that time saw race were echoed in the specific ways that racism developed in Britain after the war... Even now, surveys suggest that a large portion of British people believe that certain races were born to work harder than others. Those attitudes go straight back to empire.'

Making amends?

Furthermore, there are people alive today who suffered during the era of empire, such as those who were displaced by the Partition of India (see pages 50–51) and survivors of torture by the British army during the Mau Mau Rebellion in Kenya in the 1950s (see pages 92–93). For many of these people, and their families, the legacy of pain and trauma continues.

Some people are demanding that former colonial powers (such as Britain and France, for example) should pay reparations for the role they played in colonialism and the enslavement of millions of people. When the trade in enslaved Africans was abolished in the British Empire, for example, reparations were paid, but to the plantation owners not to the enslaved people. The debate is complicated and ongoing.

▼ **SOURCE F** From a 2022 interview with author Aanchal Malhotra, who interviewed 130 survivors of Partition, and their families. These families are still affected by the trauma caused when 15 million people were forced from their homes during Partition.

'Many interviewees made mention of the fact that their grandparents hoarded food or other items. There are also stories of grandchildren who have seen their grandparents sleep with knives under their pillows, perhaps stemming from a survival instinct developed during the days of Partition.'

Big Question

Key Words   white supremacy   reparations

In 2022, it was reported that the governments of Barbados and Jamaica were seeking reparations from Richard Drax, who is the descendent of one of the first slave-owning families in Barbados. The family still has links to Barbados and owns a plantation there. It has been suggested that part of the Drax plantation should be used to build houses for low-income families and that the family should pay some of the costs.

Unfinished business?

Many British museums, stately homes and country houses contain items that were removed – or looted – from former colonies. Some argue that these should be returned to their country of origin. In 2022, Cambridge University agreed to return over 100 precious bronze statues to Nigeria. The 'Benin Bronzes' were taken by British soldiers from the Royal Palace in Benin City in 1897. The British Museum in London has over 900 objects originating from Benin which have not been returned.

▶ **SOURCE G** One of the looted Benin Bronzes that Cambridge University will return to Nigeria. This statue is the commemorative head of the Oba, or king.

Over to You

1 Write a sentence or two to explain what is meant by the word 'legacy'.

2 Look at **Sources A**, **B**, **C**, **D**, **F** and **G**. Explain how each of these demonstrates the 'legacy of the British Empire'.

3 Suggest reasons why the legacy of the British Empire is such a complex topic.

Glossary

Aboriginal peoples the groups or nations of Indigenous Australian people from mainland Australia and Tasmania

bison a large mammal that roamed the plains of North America in large herds

boycotting a refusal to buy goods or services from a person or organisation as a protest

colony an area or country controlled by another country; for example, Britain controlled a huge number of colonies, which made up its empire

dependency another word for a colony

dominion an area with a degree of self-governance, but still part of an empire

economist a person who studies how money is made and spent

exploit to take and use something unfairly for your own advantage

guerilla warfare fast-moving, small-scale actions including ambushes, sabotage and raids

imperialism the policy of extending a country's power, influence, wealth and territory through colonisation

Indigenous peoples the first nations of people who lived in any region or country, and not later invaders, settlers or immigrants; they may continue to live in a particular country or region

legacy a situation that exists now because of events, actions and so on that took place in the past

missionary someone who travels, often abroad, to spread their religious faith

mother country the country that controls an empire

multicultural made up of people from a number of different cultures

mutiny the act of refusing to follow the orders of a person in authority

nomadic moving from one place to another, instead of living in one place

oral history the history and culture of a people passed on through storytelling from person to person, rather than being written down

partition the separation of two or more things or areas from each other

plantation a huge farm that grows cotton, sugar, tobacco and so on; plantation owners normally used enslaved people to do the work

protectorate another word for a colony

Renaissance a rebirth in learning that began in the 1400s

reparations financial payments or other compensation, given to make amends for suffering or loss caused in the past

Sepoy an Indian soldier serving British authorities

superior higher, above or better

taxed when an extra charge or fee is added on to the cost of something, usually by a government or authority

Torres Strait Islander peoples the groups or nations of Indigenous Australian people who are from – or trace their heritage from – the Torres Strait Islands to the north of Australia

totem pole a carved and painted pole that can represent a family or group's history, commemorate people who have died, mark important events or tell stories and legends; they often feature carvings of animals associated with the groups

trading station a large warehouse at a port where goods were stored and where trading took place

transportation a punishment; guilty criminals could be sent to a faraway land for a number of years; it also means taking someone or something from one place to another

tribe a group of people who speak the same language, have the same religion and share a similar culture

ultimatum a final demand, giving someone a choice between doing what the person giving the ultimatum wants, or facing consequences

viceroy someone who rules in another country or colony on behalf of the monarch

white supremacy the racist belief that white people are better than other groups and should have power over them

Index

A

Aboriginal Peoples, Australia 56–7, 58, 59, 60, 61, 62, 64–5, 67
see also Indigenous peoples
Afghanistan 70, 99
Africa
   Anglo-Zulu war 82–7
   in First World War 75
   independence in 90–3
   invasion of 80–1
   kingdoms of 78–9
   resistance to colonisation 81
   in Second World War 76
Akbar, Emperor 37
American War of Independence 29
Anglo-Afghan War 70
Anglo-Zulu war 82–7
anti-slavery campaign 32, 34–5
architecture
   'empire style' 54, 55, 99
   Indigenous American village 15
   temples and mosques 37, 78
Australia
   Australia Day/Invasion Day 60
   before arrival of British 56–7
   colonisation of 60, 62–5
   Cook's voyages to 58–9
   'first fleeters' 60–1
   in First World War 75
   free settlers 61
   Frontier Wars 63, 64
   independence of 66–7, 90
   Indigenous Australians 56–7, 58, 59, 60, 61, 62, 64–5, 67
   natural resources 56
   raids on British settlements 63
   in Second World War 76
   'Stolen Generations' 64

B

Belgian colonies 81
Bengal
   famine 39, 40
   partition of 46, 47
'Benin Bronzes' 101
bison 14
Boers 88–9
Bose, Subash Chandra 49
'Boston Tea Party' 28, 41
Boxer Rebellion 72
boycotting 35, 46
Britain
   benefits of empire 44, 54–5
   desire for empire 12–13
   as a global power 56
   impact of world wars 90
   migration from/to 20, 56, 98–9
   slave trade 24–7, 32
   social reforms 89
British Empire
   British enthusiasm for 54–5
   changing views on 10–11, 96–7
   cultural legacy 99
   development of 13
   economic benefits of 54
   impact on Britain 44, 54–5
   legacy of 98–101
   maps 9, 90
   origin of 16–19
   reasons to study 10–11
   rise and decline of 4, 9
   timeline 6–7
British Nationality Act 98
'British Raj' 44
'bull horns formation' 82, 83, 85
'bush medicine' 57

C

Cabot, John 17
Canada 17, 20, 21, 75, 76
Cape Colony 88, 89
Cape Town 93
Caribbean
   colonial troops 75, 76
   emigration to Britain 98
   plantations 26, 32
cave paintings 56
Cetshwayo, King 11, 82, 84, 87
China 72, 99
Christianity 42, 78, 80
Churchill, Winston 77
civil wars 93
Clarkson, Thomas 34, 35
Clive, Robert 39
cloth industry/trade 38, 45
colonies 8
   in Africa 80, 81
   in Australia 66
   granting of independence to 91
   impact of world wars 90–1
   in North America 18, 19, 20–3, 28–9
colonisation 8, 19, 22, 97, 99
   see also resistance to colonisation
Colston, Edward 11
Columbus, Christopher 15, 16, 17
concentration camps 88
convict settlers, Australia 60–1, 62
Cook, James 13, 58–9
Cross, Ulric 74
culture
   Africa 78, 101
   India 37, 44, 55
   Indigenous Americans 15
   Indigenous Australians 56, 57
   legacy of British Empire 99
   repatriation of cultural objects 101

D

Declaration of Independence, US 29
dependencies 8
disease 22, 64
'divide and rule' strategy 46
dominions 8

E

East India Company (EIC) 38–41, 42
Easter Rising 72–3
economists 33
Elizabeth I 18, 26
empire-building 8–9, 13, 80
English language 100
environment, impact of empire 100
Equiano, Olaudah 34
exploration 13, 16, 17, 18

F

famines 39, 40, 45, 77
farming 14, 20, 24, 26, 56
'fire stick farming' 56
'first fleeters' 60–1
First World War 11, 44, 47, 74–5, 90
flags
   Australian Aboriginal flag 65
   Torres Strait Islander flag 65
   USA 22, 29
'flagstaff' war (Heke's War) 71
Freeman, Cathy 65
French colonies 20, 21, 81
Frontier Wars, Australia 63, 64

G

Gandhi, Mohandas 48, 49
German colonies 81
Germany 49
Ghana 78, 91, 93
Gilbert, Humphrey 18
Gold Coast 91
guerilla warfare 65, 88
Gweagal people 58

H

Haiti 33
Hawaii 59
Hawkins, John 25, 26
Heke, Hōne 71
Henry VII 16, 17
Hindus 46, 48, 50
Hong Kong 99
hunting 14, 56

I

imperialism 12
India
   before arrival of British 36–7
   cultural influences on Britain 44, 55
   'divide and rule' strategy 46
   famines 39, 40, 45, 77
   First War of Independence 42–3
   in First World War 47, 74, 75

impact of British rule 44–5
independence movement 46–9
invasion of 38–9
Partition of 50–1
rebellion against British rule 41
in Second World War 48–9, 76, 77
Indian National Army 49
Indian National Congress (INC) 46, 48, 49, 50
Indigenous peoples 8, 13, 15
Africa 80, 82
Australia 56–7, 58, 59, 60, 61, 62, 64–5, 67
cost of empire 22, 97, 99
New Zealand 11, 58, 71
North America 14, 15, 18, 19, 20, 22, 29
see also resistance to colonisation
Irish War of Independence 72–3
Isandlwana, Battle of 82, 84–5, 86
Islam 78
see also mosques; Muslims

J

Jallianwala Bagh massacre 47
Jamaican Maroons 70
Jamestown 20
Japan 49
Jinnah, Mohammed Ali 48, 50

K

Kashmir 51
Kenya 91, 92, 93, 99
Kenyatta, Jomo 92
Khan, Khudadad 74
Kikuyu people 92
Kimathi, Dedan 92
Koh-i-Noor 38

L

Lakshmibai, Rani of Jhansi 43
land-ownership, perceptions of 22
legal systems 100
Liverpool 27

M

Mali, Kingdom of 78
Mangammal, Rani 36
Māori 11, 58, 71
Maroons 70

massacres 22, 43, 47, 63
Mau Mau rebellion 92
migration from/to Britain 20, 56, 98–9
mining 62, 88
missionaries 41, 80
mosques 37, 78
'mother country' 8
Mughal Empire 36–7
Musa, Mansa 78, 79
Muslim League 48, 50
Muslims 46, 48, 50, 78

N

Nanny, Queen 70
National Congress of British West Africa 91
nationalists, Ireland 72, 73
Native Natal Contingent (NNC) 84, 85
Negi, Darwan Singh 47
New Zealand 11, 58, 71, 75, 76, 90
Nigeria 93, 101
Nkrumah, Kwame 91
nomadic people 14, 56
non-violent protest 48
North America
before arrival of British 14–15
colonies in 18, 19, 20–3, 28–9
exploration of 17
indigenous peoples 14, 15, 18, 19, 20, 22, 29
plantations 26
revolution 28–9
Northern Ireland 73

O

opium trade 38, 72
oral history 15

P

Paika Bidroh (Paika Rebellion) 41
Pakistan 50, 51, 99
Pemulwuy 63
'Pilgrim Fathers' 23
plantations 26, 32, 101
Portugal 16, 81
Prince, Mary 34
protectorates 8
Puritans 23

Q

Quit India movement 49

R

racism 29, 33, 34, 92, 96, 100–1
railways 44, 45
Renaissance 16
reparations debate 101
resistance to colonisation
Afghanistan 70
Africa 81, 92
Australia 63
China 72
India 41
Ireland 72–3
Jamaica 70
New Zealand 71
North America 20
Rhodes, Cecil 96–7
Roanoke Island 18, 19
Roman empire 8
Rorke's Drift, defence of 82, 84, 85, 86, 87
Royal African Company 26
Royal Navy 33
Royal Pavilion, Brighton 99
Rudd, Kevin 64

S

Salt March 48
Second Anglo-Boer War 88–9
Second World War 48–9, 74, 76–7, 90
Sepoys 42, 43
Seven Years War 20, 21
slave revolts 24, 33
slave ships 24, 35
slave trade 24–7
abolition of 32–5
compensation of former slave owners 33, 35
profits from 26, 27
'slave triangle' 25
slavery 17, 24, 29
smallpox 64
Smith, Adam 33
social reforms, in Britain 89
South Africa 76, 89, 90, 93
Spanish colonies 21, 81
Spanish Empire 9, 16, 24
sport 100
statues, controversies about 10, 11, 17, 39, 96
'Stolen Generations' 64
sugar boycotts 35
superiority, colonists' belief in 22, 42, 96
Swadeshi movement 46–7

T

taxation 28, 38, 40, 41
tea trade 41, 54
temples 37
timelines 6–7, 66–7
Torres Strait Islander peoples 56, 59, 65
torture 92
totem poles 14
Toussaint L'Ouverture 33
trade 13, 15, 19, 38, 39, 41, 54
see also slave trade
trading stations 38, 39
transport networks 44, 45, 99
transportation (punishment) 60–1, 62

U

ultimatum 83
Unaipon, David 65
unionists, Ireland 72, 73
USA
flag of 22, 29
formation of 29
Indigenous peoples in 22
see also North America

V

viceroys 43, 46, 48, 50
Victoria, Queen 42, 44
Virginia 18, 19

W

warfare
American War of Independence 29
Anglo-Afghan War 70
Anglo-Zulu war 82–7
civil wars 93
and empire-building 13
Frontier Wars, Australia 63, 64
guerilla warfare 65, 88
Kashmir conflict 51
Second Anglo-Boer War 88
warriors, Zulu 83
West Africa Squadron 33
white supremacy 100, 101
see also racism
'Windrush Generation' 98
women, in anti-slavery groups 35

Z

Zulu war 82–7